WOMEN'S SPORTS SHORTS

WOMEN'S SPORTS SHORTS

1,001 SLAM-DUNK ONE-LINERS BY AND ABOUT WOMEN IN SPORTS

GLENN LIEBMAN

CB

CONTEMPORARY BOOKS

Library of Congress Cataloging-in-Publication Data

Liebman, Glenn.
    Women's sports shorts : 1,001 slam-dunk one-liners by and
about women in sports / Glenn Liebman.
        p.   cm.
    ISBN 0-8092-2533-6
    1. Women athletes—Quotations, maxims, etc.   I. Title.
GV709 .L54 2000
796'.082—dc21

                                                    99-55607
                                                    CIP

Jacket illustration copyright © Mark Anderson
Jacket design by Todd Petersen

Published by Contemporary Books
A division of NTC/Contemporary Publishing Group, Inc.
4255 West Touhy Avenue, Lincolnwood (Chicago), Illinois 60712-1975 U.S.A.
Copyright © 2000 by Glenn Liebman
Printed in the United States of America
International Standard Book Number: 0-8092-2533-6

00 01 02 03 04 05 LB 18 17 16 15 14 13 12 11 10 9 8 7 6 5 4 3 2 1

To my mother-in-law, Helen Coll:
Thank-you for being such a wonderful
friend, mother, and grandmother.

ACKNOWLEDGMENTS

For many of the other books in the Shorts series, I tended to go on and on with my thanks. This time I will keep it short and to the point. I'd like to thank the wonderful triumvirate at NTC/Contemporary—John Nolan, Denise Betts, and Craig Bolt. All, as always, have been exceedingly helpful throughout the process. I would also like to thank my agent, Philip Spitzer, and his assistant Jill Grosjean.

Finally, I would like to thank the two people who make everything worthwhile—my son, Frankie, and my wife, Kathy. To Frankie, the five-year-old wise guy who makes each day an adventure, whether we are superheroes saving the world from the likes of the Joker or explorers climbing the huge two-foot mountain in our backyard. And to Kathy, who has the love, humor, and patience to deal with a real five-year-old and a forty-one-year-old who *thinks* he is a five-year-old.

INTRODUCTION

I don't come from a family of athletes, unless you count my second-place finish in the fifty-yard dash in my fifth-grade Olympics (my crowning moment as an athlete). My wife, on the other hand, comes from a family of accomplished athletes—almost all of them female.

Both my wife and mother-in-law competed as race walkers in the Empire State Games (New York's version of the Olympics) for several years. My sister-in-law Bridget won a gold medal in swimming at the Empire State Games. She now consistently wins medals as a Masters swimmer. Another sister-in-law, Laura, is a world-class runner who has competed in the Olympic trials.

Being around these female athletes has given me a different perspective on sports (unfortunately, however, it hasn't motivated me to do anything athletic). That is why I am not surprised by how the landscape has dramatically changed for female athletics in recent years. It is wonderful to witness.

Whether it's the women's soccer or hockey team or individuals such as Marion Jones or Lindsay Davenport, it is clear that women have taken their rightful place alongside men in sports. It would not surprise me in five years to see my then-ten-year-old son place his Chamique Holdsclaw–autographed basketball next to his Grant Hill–autographed ball. Chronicling these changes through humorous ("We don't even get the quality clowns"—Lynn Jankowski, on the difference between men's and women's rodeo), uplifting ("Now it's cool for a women to be able to out–bench press her husband"—Amy Van Dyken), and sometimes poignant ("I want a little boy to say, forty years from now, 'I want to run like Marion Jones, not Carl Lewis or Michael Johnson.'"—Marion Jones) one-liners has been a delightful experience. Enjoy the book!

WOMEN'S SPORTS SHORTS

"She's no spring chicken, but she can haul."
> *Darlene Bechford, on 36-year-old*
> *Maricica Puica, Olympic 3,000-*
> *meters gold medalist*

"By then I'll be 74—just two over par."
> *Patty Berg, legendary golfer, on being*
> *told it would take her two years to*
> *fully recover from back surgery*

"Steffi's so nice. And she's not an old person. She
wears an MTV shirt."
> *Jennifer Capriati, on 21-year-old*
> *Steffi Graf*

"Reincarnation."
> *Rosie Casals, on how she made it to*
> *the fourth round of Wimbledon at an*
> *old age*

"You see these kids with their entourages—fathers, coaches, people trailing the kids to wipe their noses and clean their diapers."

Bud Collins, on the young phenoms in women's tennis

"Heidi and Lolita do the U.S. Open."

Bud Collins, on 15-year-old Martina Hingis playing 15-year-old Anna Kournikova

"I'm only 14."

Nadia Comaneci, asked after winning the gold medal if she was going to retire

"Her idea of drug use is probably Flintstone vitamins."

Mike Downey, columnist, on 14-year-old Olympic swimmer Amanda Beard

"We're so young, we decided to dress only seven players on the road. We're pretty confident the other five can dress themselves."

> *Charlie Just, women's basketball*
> *coach at Bellarmine College, on his*
> *very young team*

"My body has pretty much told me that it's given everything it's going to give."

> *Francie Larrieu Smith, on*
> *slowing down after years as*
> *a topflight runner*

"I act my age better than she does."

> *Carl Lindgren, 84 years old, on his*
> *86-year-old wife, Mavis, who had just*
> *completed a marathon*

"I guess you get slower as you get older."

> *Mavis Lindgren, 87-year-old*
> *marathoner, on having slower times*
> *than in previous years*

"Stop playing against the girls and start fighting against the women."

> *Mirjana Lucie, on joining the pro*
> *tennis tour at age 15*

"I'll be able to show people it doesn't matter how old you are."

> *Shannon Miller, on being labeled too old for gymnastics at age 19*

"Should van Gogh have stopped painting at an early age?"

> *Martina Navratilova, asked if she considered retirement after winning her 10th Wimbledon*

"The only thing I like about that number is that it's a good score to turn in for nine holes."

> *Liselotte Neumann, LPGA pro, on turning 30*

"It's not do or die; it's do or don't."

> *Merlene Ottey, track star, on her future at age 37*

"I guess I could put it on one of my jackets, but I think at my age I will frame it and put it in the hallway where everyone can see it."

Vera Ratts, 89 years old, on being given an honorary letter from the Indiana University swim team because when she was competing, they did not give women varsity letters

"Of course, I can say, individually I hate them."

Alice Ritzman, LPGA nonwinner, on the new stars of the game

"You lose a lot of speed between 80 and 86."

Ruth Rothfarb, on having one of her slower times when running in her late 80s

"If you drive a Porsche or Mercedes at 17, what the heck will you have left to drive when you're 30?"

Pam Shriver, on large purses for women tennis pros

"This is the first time I've fulfilled the fantasy of a middle-aged man."

> *Pam Shriver, on beating a middle-aged man in tennis in a Play the Pro contest*

"I don't know where they're coming from, but I wish they'd send them back."

> *Wendy Turnbull, pro tennis player, on losing to young, talented players*

"I want to show people that we're not just a bunch of old ladies out there running. We're going pretty fast."

> *Ruth Wysocki, on Masters runners*

"It's hard to keep up with the younger people coming up."

> *Kim Zmeskal, 16-year-old gymnast*

ADS

"It didn't take much courage; it was nothing compared with how you feel on the starting line of a championship race."

Suzy Hamilton, professional runner, on appearing nude in a Nike ad

"It was paint. They were worried it might come off. I was more worried it might not come off."

Amy Van Dyken, Olympic swimmer, on being filmed underwater with a milk mustache for a "Got Milk?" ad

AIR FLIGHT

"But I can't seem to get anything. I seem to get stiffed by all the airline companies."

Laura Davies, LPGA golf pro, on qualifying for five different frequent-flyer programs

"Toughest goddamn player I ever played with."
> *Brandi Chastain, soccer teammate*

"From someone who knows how to take a hit, I really admire you."
> *President Clinton, to Akers after an injury had forced her to leave the World Cup championship game*

"The fans were treated to witnessing one of the greatest women athletes in history, a true champion."
> *Tony DiCicco, U.S. World Cup team coach*

"They feel like cannonballs when you catch them."
> *Tony DiCicco, on Akers's shot*

"Talking about the history of the game with Michelle Akers is like discussing the Constitutional Convention with James Madison."
> *Grant Wahl*

ALL—STAR GAME

"My mom may have realized you can vote more than once."

> *Rebecca Lobo, on being voted to the WNBA All-Star team despite missing most of the season because of an injury*

AMATEURS

"I'm a professional in Europe. I'm treated that way. I'm used to being a star. And then I come back home, and I'm treated like an amateur."

> *Bridgette Gordon, U.S. Olympic basketball player, on playing professionally in Italy*

ANATOMY

"Hey, I ran my ass off for this body. I'm proud of it."

> *Brandi Chastain, U.S. soccer star, on*
> *appearing seminude in a magazine*

"How does he know? He doesn't have any."

> *Nancy Lopez, professional golfer,*
> *on Ben Wright's comments that*
> *women golfers are handicapped*
> *by their "boobs"*

ARCHERY

"I try to have no emotion about what happens to the arrow. I just concentrate on my form."

> *Janet Dykman, U.S. Olympic archer,*
> *on using zen in her sport*

TRACY AUSTIN

"When Tracy was eight, she would beat the best ladies at the local tennis club and then go over to the baby-sitting area and play in the sandbox."
Jeanne Austin, mother of Tracy

"Tracy's mental strength was scary. She had no weaknesses. She was obsessed about winning."
Chris Evert

AUTO RACING

"You drive the car; you don't carry it."
Janet Guthrie, on the importance of strength in auto racing

"I want to be the fastest woman in the world— in a manner of speaking."
Shirley Muldowney, speed racer

"I love racing. I truly know that the gratification I get from driving is absolutely necessary in my life."

> *Lyn St. James, first female racer in the Indianapolis 500*

"You have to win by the rules. Then, when you win enough, you can begin to change the rules."

> *Lyn St. James*

AUTOGRAPHS

"I buy a bagel somewhere, and they run after me in the parking lot [for an autograph]. It's crazy and I love it."

> *Michelle Akers, U.S. Olympic soccer star, on the excitement of the fans for the U.S. Olympic soccer team of 1996*

"What's really exciting is not just the little girls asking for my autographs, but the little boys. As I see it, if a little boy asks for my autograph, maybe he'll treat a girl a little bit differently."

> *Rebecca Lobo, basketball star*

AWARDS

"I thought you had to be dead to win that."
>JoAnne Carner, on winning the
>Bob Jones sportsmanship award

"What are you trying to do, make a housewife out of me?"
>Martina Hingis, on winning the
>Hoover Vacuum clean sweep award

BACKHAND

"When she got good at it, why should I change it?"
>Jimmy Evert, on why he never
>changed daughter Chris's
>two-handed backhand

"Tara Lipinski does more jumps. I don't do so many jumps. But artistry makes a difference. The fact Tara has lost twice this season proves the judges have had enough of childish skating."

> *Maria Butryskaya, Soviet skater,*
> *prior to Tara Lipinski's winning the*
> *gold medal in the '98 Olympics*

OKSANA BAIUL

"I skate how I feel. I think it must be a gift from God."

> *Oksana Baiul*

"Every once in a while, a diamond falls into the lap of the skating world."

> *Sandra Bezic, skating commentator*

"When Oksana presents a program, you can see it coming from the heart—from inside."

> *Britta Lindgren, skating official, on*
> *Baiul's 1994 gold medal performance*

BASEBALL

"I don't want to be a cause, and I don't think I am one; I umpire because I love the game."

Pam Postema, minor-league umpire
who came close to making it to the
major leagues

BASKETBALL WISDOM

"We don't exactly have Phi Beta Kappas in this league."

Nancy Lieberman, on playing in the
U.S. Basketball League

"It's more of a team sport. You can watch the strategy evolve over the course of a game."

Pat Summitt, on women's basketball
versus men's basketball

"The WBL is great. It gives women like me who don't want to work something to do."

Linnell Jones, on the defunct World
Basketball League

"Maybe soon, on career days, little girls will be saying they want to be a basketball player."
Lisa Leslie

"People in this country don't realize that the best women's basketball is played after college."
Katrina McClain, 1996 U.S. Olympic basketball team player

"I wasn't the greatest athlete, and I couldn't jump out of the gym, and I wasn't an extraordinary ball handler. I was just someone who loved the game."
Cheryl Miller, on being inducted into the Basketball Hall of Fame

"My main purpose was to go in as a ballplayer, to hold my head up and do my best."
Ann Meyers, on being the first woman invited to an NBA tryout camp

"The women in basketball are playing for the sheer joy and love of the game. . . . People are sick of seeing men's pro sports where millionaires are bickering with billionaires."
Robin Roberts

"We're playing a man-to-man defense. Person-to-person sounds like a phone call."

> *Vincent Tralka, women's high school basketball coach*

"The difference here is that the players smell so much nicer and you see hair rollers in the locker room."

> *Butch van Breda Koff, former NBA coach, on coaching a women's basketball team*

"The best pure basketball I see today is from some of the better women's teams."

> *John Wooden, 1996*

BATTLE OF THE SEXES

"An old, obnoxious has-been like Riggs who can't hear, can't see, walks like a duck, and is an idiot besides."

> *Rosie Casals, on Billie Jean King's opponent, Bobby Riggs*

"I've always said Bobby Riggs did more for women's tennis than anybody."

> *Rosie Casals, on King's defeat of Riggs*

"It meant something because she won."

> *Frank Deford*

"Billie Jean went from Riggs to riches."

> *Bob Hope*

"I kept thinking this was not about a tennis match, this was about social change."

> *Billie Jean King*

"Before that, women were chokers and spastics who couldn't take pressure. Except, of course, in childbirth."

> *Billie Jean King, on the significance of the match*

"When I got back to the hotel, I had about 30 ice cream sundaes delivered to my room."

> *Billie Jean King, on her reward for winning the match*

"I'll tell you why I'll win; she's a woman, and they just don't have the emotional stability."

Bobby Riggs, before the match

"Women are brought up from the time they're six years old to read books, eat candy, and go to dance class. They can't compete against men."

Gene Scott, tennis pro, on the likelihood of a Riggs victory

"On campuses, people were hanging out of the dorm rooms celebrating. The match had enormous symbolic importance."

Gloria Steinem

BIKING

"I'm a mountain goat. I have climbing power. I can win going away."

Jeannie Longo, bicycling champion from France, on biking in the mountains

BIRDIES

"God knew I couldn't putt, so He put me close to the tee."

> *Barbara Barrow, on winning an*
> *LPGA event with five birdies on the*
> *last nine holes*

BONNIE BLAIR

"Trying to summarize all of Bonnie Blair's accomplishments is like attempting to squeeze the Declaration of Independence onto a note card."
> *Anonymous*

"She brings out the best in her competition, because we're always out chasing her."
> *Susan Auch, fellow speed skater*

"A lot of people want to drive by his house [Michael Jordan] and see where he lives. But you don't think of that for a speed skater. . . . It just doesn't seem to fit."

Bonnie Blair, on a couple that came a long distance to visit her house

"I look at her like some kind of speed-skating goddess."

Mary Docter, fellow speed skater

"It's hard to describe Bonnie. She's just a tough chick."

Mary Docter

"I don't have to teach her much. I just keep her head fresh, get her in condition, and let Bonnie be Bonnie."

Peter Mueller, Blair's coach

"It's like she was born on the ice."

Peter Mueller

"I have never felt like we were in the shadow of our men. I have always felt like our men's basketball program casts a light on us and our entire university."

Gail Goestenkors, coach of Duke's 1999 NCAA finals women's basketball team

SVETLANA BOGINSKAYA

"She who is beautiful is a pleasure to watch."

Aleksandr Aleksandrov, gymnastics coach, on Boginskaya's enduring legacy as a gymnast

BOOK REVIEW

"I thought it was a pretty good book. It made me look pretty good, actually, for the mean SOB I am."

Jimmy Connors, on Chris Evert's autobiography

BOXING

"She is not a woman the moment she steps in the ring with me. When she steps in the ring with me, she's an opponent."

Loi Chow, before fighting Margaret McGregor in the first-ever man versus woman professional boxing match

"It's a lot harder than tennis. If *I* make a mistake, it's 0–15. In boxing, you let your head down once and you're in the hospital."

Andrea Jaeger

"This isn't a matter of men looking for some weird sexual thrill. It's women supporting women athletes."

>*Rick Kulis, producer, on why*
>*television ratings increase for*
>*female boxing matches*

"I don't look at it as [being female] in a male-dominated sport, because I'm not trying to fight a man. I'm just competing against a woman."

>*Christy Martin, champion boxer*

"My passion for boxing is so great that sometimes at the end of the fight, I even forget to pick up my paycheck."

>*Mia Rosale St. John,*
>*professional boxer*

"A woman's body shouldn't be hit in the stomach. Women's bodies are built to reproduce."

>*Emanuel Stewart, Hall of Fame*
>*boxing trainer*

BOYCOTTS

"I'm going to tell them an Olympic champion is an Olympic champion, no matter who shows up. That gold medal is still a gold medal. Nobody is going to remember who didn't show up."

Don Gambril, women's U.S. Olympic swim coach, on the 1984 games which were boycotted by several Eastern European countries

"I'd think twice about going to Russia. Of course, it's easy for me to say, an old broad who had her day."

Eleanor Holm, gold medalist in the 1932 Olympics, on the U.S. boycott of the 1980 Olympics

PAT BRADLEY

"Death, taxes, and Pat Bradley on the leaders board."

Val Skinner, LPGA pro, on the three things you can count on in life

"Pat Bradley is a great player, but what can you say about Pat Bradley but what she shot? All she does is practice and play."

Jan Stephenson

BREAKFAST OF CHAMPIONS

"What really counts is that she eats nails for breakfast."

> *Peter Carruthers, on the toughness of his sister and skating partner Kitty, who is only 5'1"*

"I don't even like Wheaties."

> *Phoebe Mills, U.S. gymnast, downplaying her expectations as a star athlete*

"They're all going to celebrate by eating a cornflake."

> *Hubert Mizell, columnist, after the U.S. women gymnasts won the bronze medal in the '92 Olympics*

"I'm happy as a pig in mud on a cross-country course."

> *Lynn Jennings, on winning the*
> *bronze in the 10,000 in the*
> *'92 Olympics*

"Bronze does not shine as bright as gold. But for me, it shines the most."

> *Tomomi Okazaki, on winning a*
> *bronze medal in speed skating in*
> *the '98 Olympics*

"I don't want to be the woman of bronze, but the lady of gold."

> *Merlene Ottey, Jamaican sprinter, on*
> *always finishing third in major events*

"In my heart, it's worth gold."

> *Annie Pelletier, on winning a*
> *surprising bronze medal in diving*
> *in the '96 Olympics*

"She was such a beautiful player. I used to watch her play and not watch the ball at all."

Francoise Durr, on the elegance of Bueno's tennis

CADDIES

"I don't know why that putt hung on the edge. I'm a clean liver. It must be my caddie."

JoAnne Carner

"I couldn't figure it out. I wore deodorant and everything."

Marlene Hagge, LPGA pro, on having five different caddies in one day

"The way Betsy was playing, Rin Tin Tin could carry her clubs and it wouldn't make any difference."

Gary Morrison, on being credited for helping Betsy King shoot a 65

"He's still caddying for me. He carries the bag from the trunk of the car to the golf course."

Nancy Lopez, on firing her husband, former major-league baseball player Ray Knight, as her caddie

MARY CARILLO

"She's my idol. She's blunt and abrasive, but she's honest. I'm trying to be as good as she is."

Chris Evert, on Carillo's television style

JOANNE CARNER

"When JoAnne joined the LPGA tour, they were playing with hickory shafts."

Tammie Green, poking fun at her friend on turning 60

TRACY CAULKINS

"This has been the highlight of my life. This silver is just as good as gold considering who I was swimming behind. I'm on cloud 900."

> *Nancy Hogshead, on finishing*
> *second to Caulkins in the 200-meter*
> *individual medley in '84*

CHAMPIONS

"Whenever I hear anyone call me champ, I think there's something behind it."

> *Althea Gibson, former tennis great*

"If you are the champion of the world, you can't take much pleasure in it, or otherwise you couldn't be the best."

> *Billie Jean King*

"But the role I like best is champion."

> *Katarina Witt, on her preferred role*
> *after winning her second skating*
> *gold medal*

CHARACTER FLAWS

"Actually, the person who stands out the most in my mind for jerky behavior is me."

> *Pam Shriver, asked who in tennis stands out for worst behavior*

CHAUVINISTS

"My wife is a real housewife. She cooks, cleans and takes care of our children. She sews and knits their clothes."

> *Husband of Fanny Blankers-Koen, track star who won four gold medals in the '48 Olympics*

"Two percent is enough."

> *Walter Byers, former NCCA executive director, on being told in 1974 that only 2 percent of the NCAA budget went for women's sports*

"Two sets of rubbish that last only half an hour."
Pat Cash, tennis pro, on women's tennis

"There is no girl living who can manage to look anything but awful during the process of some strenuous game played on a hot day."
Paul Gallico, sportswriter, 1936

"Martina couldn't even beat her own coach (Mike Estep). If Estep (at age 35) came back on tour, he'd be ranked 2,000."
Vitas Gerulaitis, on women's tennis and Martina Navratilova

"You can bet your ass if you have women around— and I've talked to psychiatrists about this—you aren't going to be worth a damn. . . . Man has to dominate."
Woody Hayes, on Oberlin College's having a women's sports program

"They pushed me away like I wasn't there. My coach says, 'You are like a girl.'"

> *Arturas Karnishovas, forward on the Lithuanian Olympic basketball team, on being dominated by the U.S. Olympic Dream Team*

"It's the boxers who attract the real women, after all, with their raw primeval strength, beautifully toned bodies, and just a touch of vulnerability."

> *Eamon McCabe, British journalist*

"I'm not sure the men would really know the women's game. I mean, how do you know exactly how the women are feeling certain times of the month?"

> *John McEnroe, on men announcing women's tennis*

"I think women are too emotional to be any good around the greens in the clutch."

> *Bob Rosburg, former golf pro*

"That's why I marry her."

Oscar Schmidt, Brazilian basketball star, on his wife's practicing with him by passing him the ball up to a thousand times a day

"He shouldn't pick on girls just because he hasn't had much luck with guys."

Pam Shriver, on the chauvinistic statements of the late Vitas Gerulaitis

"I haven't watched women's tennis in 20 years, and I have no intention to watch for the next 20."

Ion Tiriac, former tennis pro and coach, asked about a women's tennis match

"Men are made differently than women. Men compete, get along, and move on, with few emotions. But women break down, get emotional."

Mike Tranghese, Big East basketball commissioner

"Listen, I like to go out with chicks as much as anybody. Maybe more. But I didn't see too many in the league I'd date."

Butch van Breda Koff, former coach in the Women's Basketball League

CHEATING

"I feel like I was stopped on the highway, robbed, kicked in the mouth, and then you go home naked."

Bela Karolyi, U.S. women's gymnastics coach, attributing his team's losing half a point to cheating by some judges

CHEERLEADERS

"These women—are they wayward?"

Viktor Tikhanov, Russian hockey coach, after seeing cheerleaders for the first time in a professional football game

CHINA

"You figure there's eight trillion people in China: and if she was number one there, it says something."

Pam Shriver, on barely beating her opponent, Hu Na, of China

COACHES

"Rooter. I am going to get some pom-poms and just get out there."

JoAnne Carner, women's coach of the U.S. Solheim Cup golf team, on her role on opening day

"I've got a headache, and I'm ready for a Stoli."

JoAnne Carner, after her first day as coach of the team

"My mother is a loving, gentle person. She taught me to be compassionate. . . . I want to be like my mom off the court and my dad on the court."
Pat Summitt, legendary women's basketball coach

COLLEGE YEARS

"Our goal at USC is to play like men on the court and behave like women off the court."
Cheryl Miller

"They wanted me to write about a meaningful experience in my life. I wanted to write them back and say, 'Hey, could you wait two months . . . I'm going to the Olympics."
Angela Ruggiero, Olympic hockey star, on filling out her college applications

"There has never been anyone like her, never been anyone who approaches her."

> *Frank Bare, U.S. Gymnastics*
> *Foundation executive director, on*
> *Comaneci's performance in the*
> *'76 Olympics*

"Nadia was a super-pressure performer. It was as if 'This child doesn't care for me; I better admire her.'"

> *Bela Karolyi*

"Nadia Comaneci flew through the air like a flight of doves off a backwoods lake when the sun hits it."

> *Jim Murray*

COMPETITION

"A lot of great players don't win Super Bowls."

> *Amy Benz, LPGA pro, on playing*
> *more than 300 events without a win*

"To me, to race is to go all out, every time."
Bonnie Blair

"Determining figure-skating winners is like judging
wine: you so enjoy the competition, you hope to
never have to make a decision."
Dick Button

"Competition is even more fun than golf. I like
going down to the wire knowing somebody's going
to choke and hoping it's not me."
JoAnne Carner

"I attacked my weaker opponents more furiously
than any other girl in the history of tennis."
Maureen Connolly

"This was no passing dislike, but a blazing,
virulent, powerful, and consuming hate. I believed
I could not win without hatred."
Maureen Connolly

"I didn't give a darn who was on the other side
of the net; I'd knock you down if you got in
the way."

Althea Gibson

"It's just the playing, you being on court, that keeps me going. That's what matters."
> *Steffi Graf, on playing through adversity at age 29*

"Big boys, small boys, whoever—I was always ready to take them on. I wasn't scared of anybody's game."
> *Chamique Holdsclaw*

"I always feel big and powerful, like a draft horse, next to little women on the starting line."
> *Lynn Jennings*

"Get out and go do . . . agriculture."
> *Bela Karolyi, on a Romanian judge with whom he disagreed during a competition*

"Each point I play is the now moment: the last point means nothing; the next point means nothing."
> *Billie Jean King*

"When you're up there [on the leaders board], you win some and you lose some, but the fun of it is to have a chance in the last round."

Betsy King, LPGA pro

"That's where I feel most free. That's where I can do exactly what I want."

Nancy Lopez, on being inside the ropes

"Put it this way: it's much better for me if she wins."

Michael Marx, on his wife, Leslie, a fellow Olympic fencer

"I think the difference between me and other guys is that a lot of them don't have, truly don't have, the kick-ass attitude."

Shirley Muldowney, champion race car driver

"They don't really look at me as the woman driver anymore, but what devastates them is that a woman whips their asses."

Shirley Muldowney

"I am glad she is confident about beating me, but talk does not scare me. Do it with a racket, please."

> *Martina Navratilova, on Hana Mandilokova's saying she could beat her*

"I never think about anybody. I let them think about me."

> *Wyomia Tyus, sprinter, on being nervous about her competition*

"When I stopped competing . . . I started venturing in other areas. I looked at my husband, and I'd be like, 'I can make a pancake bigger and faster than you.'"

> *Amy Van Dyken, Olympic swimmer, on her competitive nature*

"When I get ready to swim, I might bite your head off if you joke with me."

> *Amy Van Dyken*

"When I'm swimming against someone, I want her to drown."

> *Janie Wagstaff, U.S. Olympic swimmer*

"I'm trying to think of whom I should lose to and why, and I can't think of any reasons why I should."

Venus Williams

COMPLAINT DEPARTMENT

"When we complain about conditions, we're just bitches. But when the men complain, people think, 'Well, it really must be hard.'"

Betsy King, LPGA pro

CONFIDENCE

"You know you're better than the other players because there are so many times when you're down 5–3 in the third set and you don't get worried."

Chris Evert, on her confidence as a player

"Just the confidence that comes with chasing a dream and having it come through will make you feel you can do anything."

Sarah Tueting, Olympic hockey goalie, on the Olympic experience

CONSISTENCY

"I don't want streaks. I want a Hall of Fame speech one day. Careers aren't built on streaks."

Dottie Pepper, on going through a hot streak on the LPGA tour

CYNTHIA COOPER

"Coop can shoot, rebound, pass, and guard the best players. I'm in awe."

Van Chancellor, Cooper's coach on the Houston Comets

"The toughest thing about guarding her is that most of the time you know exactly what she's going to do, but you still can't stop her. She's incredible."
Crystal Robinson, WNBA player

COURSES

"This course is so tight, it squeaks."
Connie Chillemi, LPGA pro, on the narrow fairways at Bethesda Country Club

CRITICS

"I step up and embrace (critics), because it's just another challenge. It fuels my fire."
Shannon Miller, Canadian women's hockey coach, on her many critics

DANCING MACHINE

"But, I'll leave my shirt on."

> *Ruth Wysocki, joking about repeating*
> *the end-zone dance of a U.S. high*
> *jumper if she won the 1,500*

BETH DANIELS

"I have always looked up to Beth both as a player and physically she is a lot taller than I am."

> *Patty Sheehan*

DATING GAME

"Anybody over 6'3"."

> *Lindsay Davenport, who is 6'2", on*
> *whom she wants to date*

"I don't date, but if Leonardo DiCaprio is free . . ."

Michelle Kwan, on her lack of a social life because of her skating regimen

"I normally date guys who play basketball and who are taller than I am."

Lisa Leslie, asked if men were intimidated by her being 6'5"

"Here I am an Olympic champion; boys can wait—not too long, but they can wait."

Mary Lou Retton, on her lack of a social life because of all her training

"I don't want some macho junk-jock guy, but I don't want him to be a wimp. And he can't be tall either."

Kerri Strug, Olympic gymnast, on what she is looking for in a man

"Somebody has to start a trend."

Katarina Witt, on being told by Donald Trump that she was the only person given his private number who never called him

LINDSAY DAVENPORT

"I don't wear braids or say I'm going to be number one. I like to do my talking with my racket."

Lindsay Davenport, on her off-court demeanor

"It's not so much Lindsay's size. It's the way she hits the ball—so hard you don't have any say in it."

Amanda Coetzer

"It moves, curves like a baseball. You get there, then wonder, where's the ball?"

Martina Hingis, on the way Davenport hits the ball

LAURA DAVIES

"I can only dream of hitting it as far as she does."

Donna Andrews

"I've seen a lot of big hitters, but this girl takes the cake. They said JoAnne [Carner] was Big Momma, but this young lady flat-out goes by all that."

Pat Bradley, LPGA pro, on the early career of Davies

"If she used a driver off the tee and kept it in the fairway, the rest of us would be playing for second most of the time."

Nancy Lopez

"She can do everything Nick Faldo can do and make sure the sun never sets on the British Empire."

Jim Murray

"She doesn't yell, 'Fore'; she yells 'Lift off.'"

Jim Murray

"She can't beat the men. She can't even beat the women now."

Lee Trevino

"I have no idea why he would want to say that, apart from the fact that he's a complete tosser [jerk] and can't play himself anymore."
Laura Davies, on Trevino's criticizing her game

DECATHLON

"It's the same old thing: they say women can't do as much as men. Officials, they never learn."
Chuck DeBus, pentathlon coach, lobbying to change the Olympic pentathlon to a decathlon like the men's

MARY DECKER

"She was the only runner I ever feared."
Francie Larrieu Smith

"When Decker runs, there isn't any second; there's another race altogether."
Jim Murray

GAIL DEVERS

"It may take awhile for the bulb to go on in Gail's head, but once it does, and she sees what she can do, she's unstoppable."

Bob Kersee, Devers's coach

BABE DIDRIKSON

"She must be Superman's sister."

Anonymous, after watching Didrikson hit a drive in the British Women's Amateur Championship

"Implausible is the adjective that best befits the Babe."

Arthur Daly

"Before I was in my teens, I knew exactly what I wanted to be: I wanted to be the best athlete who ever lived."

Babe Didrikson

"I hit the ball like a girl, and she hits it like a man."

> *Bob Hope, on Didrikson's golf game*

"The most flawless specimen of muscle harmony, of complete mental and physical coordination, the world of sports has ever known."

> *Grantland Rice*

DISHING DIRT

"I don't rise to the occasion against lesser players."

> *Pam Shriver, on her loss to*
> *Wendy Turnbull*

DISNEY WORLD

"I think she was going to be the princess of the race, because she was the first one to the castle."

> *Joan Benoit, on lagging behind*
> *Laurie Corbin until ultimately*
> *beating her in the Disney mini-*
> *marathon*

"Would you want to have to cast women as ugly stepsisters?"

> *Dorothy Hamill, on running the Ice Capades and having men portray the stepsisters in* Cinderella

"The most corniest thing I've ever done."

> *Nancy Kerrigan, on riding on a float in Disney World after the '94 Olympics*

DISSING SPICE

"It was a big deal for everyone, but not for me."

> *Anna Kournikova, tennis star, on meeting the Spice Girls*

DIVIDING LINE

"I messed up with the lines. I thought the first line was the finish. But I thought it went really well anyway."

> *Marion Jones, on winning a race but being confused by a marker before the finish line*

DIVING

"When you hit the water correctly, you feel like you're shooting through it like a missile. When you don't, you feel like you're smacking into concrete."

> *Patty Armstrong, U.S. diver, during Olympic Trials*

"Every day I don't dive, I feel like I die a little."

> *Lauren Hutton, model and actress*

"It's a contact sport. It looks so easy, but when you get up there, you're like—'OK, I'm going to throw up.'"

Wendy Williams, U.S. Olympic bronze medal winner

DOLLS

"Young women from Brooklyn to Stockholm will go to sleep at night with their soccer balls instead of their dolls."

Donna Shalala, U.S. secretary for Health and Human Services, on the impact of the U.S. soccer team in the World Cup

"I used to tear up the dolls' heads and make them into soccer balls."

Sissi, Brazilian soccer star, on refusing to play with dolls as a child

"I'd say no, I have a BB gun."

Picabo Street, on being asked as a child if she had dolls

DOUBLES

"I like to say it was his first grand-slam title and my last."

> *Mary Carillo, on winning her only*
> *grand slam playing mixed doubles*
> *with then amateur John McEnroe in*
> *the French Open*

"It's kind of like arriving for dessert."

> *Mary Carillo, on giving up singles*
> *and focusing on doubles*

DREAMS

"It's a great time to be a female athlete. I'm living a dream."

> *Cynthia Cooper*

DRIVE MY CAR

"Right now, I think she's hoping just to be able to get down and reach the pedals."

> *Mike Burg, Tara Lipinski's agent,*
> *asked if she would buy a car with all*
> *her newfound wealth at age 14*

"It's the only one in the city. I don't drive it too much, but it is a beautiful car."

> *Zoya Ivanova, after winning a*
> *Mercedes in the L.A. Marathon and*
> *taking it home to her small city in*
> *the Soviet Union*

"I have to race. I'm like a Ferrari; you can't keep it in the garage."

> *Regina Jacobs, three-time Olympian*
> *in the 1,500 meters*

"I hope to win more of them and start my own dealership."

> *Sally Little, on winning an LPGA*
> *event in which first prize was a*
> *Mazda for the second year in a row*

"It's like taking a Ferrari to the shop. We're not changing the whole engine."

> *Martina Navratilova, on fine-tuning her game*

"It's just as well I won, because if Jennifer Capriati won, she couldn't drive it anyway."

> *Martina Navratilova, after beating the 14-year-old in a tournament and winning a car*

"Yes, a Porsche."

> *Mary Lou Retton, asked if she could ask for anything more after winning the gold medal*

DRIVES

"Hitch up my girdle and let it rip."

> *Amy Alcott, on her style of golf*

"Finish high and let 'em fly."

> *Patty Berg, legendary golf pro*

"I've got a flat, quick, ugly swing, but I've saved a lot of money on lessons."

> *Dawn Coe-Jones, LPGA tour pro*

"Luckily, it was downward and with a lie. Otherwise, I'd be off being drug-tested."

> *Laura Davies, on hitting a four-iron more than 240 yards*

"That's fine, but I hit my putts as long as my drives."

> *Laura Davies, on being the longest hitter on the LPGA tour*

"Yeah, because I was stupid then."

> *Laura Davies, on using her driver early in her career for every hole*

"I still have an advantage on the par-five holes because I can reach them all in two."

> *Laura Davies*

"We have no doubt we're women."

> *Marie Pierre Guilbaud, French
> cross-country skier, on Olympic
> gender verification testing*

"It's sad that people think a drug can make you a champion. Nothing replaces hard work, faith in God, and belief in yourself."

> *Florence Griffith-Joyner, on
> allegations of steroid use*

"I must admit I was worried for a while. I have four children and eight grandchildren. I wondered what I was going to tell them—'Call me Grandpa.'?"

> *Maxine Mitchell, 51-year-old U.S.
> Olympic fencer, on gender testing*

"I was trying to figure out what I'd do if I failed. Finally, I decided I'd just call over and say, 'Hi, Ma; hi, Dad. This is your son Kate.'"

> *Kate Schmidt, U.S. Olympian, on
> fears that her ulcer medication might
> play havoc with her gender test*

DUNKS

"There's something about jumping that seems to fascinate guys. . . . Girls are more like, 'As long as the ball goes in, who cares how it got there.'"

Lisa Leslie, on men's fascination with her ability to dunk the ball

EGO

"It's all the time Tiger Woods, Tiger Woods, Tiger Woods. I am better than he is. I've been on top longer, and I am younger. I'm just better."

Martina Hingis

"If you want to know about my ego, which is obviously big, it operates this way: Every time you tell me I can't do something, that ego tells me I not only can do it, but must."

Billie Jean King

"This is good. It shows that she didn't beat me. I lost because I made all the mistakes in the match, right? That means I'm a little better than her."

Anna Kournikova, on losing a match to Venus Williams

"I can do it all—hit anything I want. I feel no fear. I deserve every bit of attention."

Anna Kournikova

"I am the great Lenglen."

Suzanne Lenglen, tennis legend, to an usher who asked to see her ticket in the 1920 Olympics

"I think I started a revolution. Before me, girls were afraid of cycling."

Jeannie Longo, Olympic cyclist

"To save themselves from embarrassment."

Ismaila Mabo, Nigerian women's soccer coach, on why South Korea would use five defenders against the offense of Nigeria

"I touch everyone. Everyone wants to see me, and I don't blame them. Got to get a look at Serena."
Serena Williams

E-MAIL

"We laugh together. I can tell when she's laughing, too. I type a little faster."
Venus Williams, on talking to her sister Serena, who was in Paris while Venus was in the United States

ETHIOPIA

"When I am running, the greatest attention is on the race. But when I see the flag of my country, I turn around and look at them and fill myself with great courage."
Fatuma Roba, from Ethiopia, on winning the Boston Marathon

"Janet will always be the queen of swimming. You know how you always hear about Mark Spitz every four years? Same way."

> *Brooke Bennett, Olympic gold medal winner, comparing herself with Evans*

"The girl has the endurance of Tarzan. If they miss the plane, she might freestyle her way home."

> *Mike Downey, columnist, on Evert's amazing performance in the 1988 Olympics in South Korea*

"She's a butt kicker with boots on."

> *Paul Evans, on daughter Janet*

"Janet Evans is in a different dimension. A swimmer like Janet comes around once every 25 years."

> *Heike Fredrick, East German swimmer*

"I'll stop short of saying Janet's a fish, but physiologically she's very similar."
> *Dr. John Troup, director of Sports Medicine for the 1988 U.S. Olympic Team*

CHRIS EVERT

"I told them I would prepare for the match: I would go to St. Patrick's."
> *Sherry Acker, on telling her friends how she would train to play Chris Evert in the U.S. Open*

"Chris Evert goes to the net every other April, but she goes to the bank every Monday."
> *Vic Braden*

"What in the world could be boring about hitting a perfect ball?"
> *Mary Carillo, on Evert's game being called boring*

"Chris is so great because when she misses, she looks around as if something is wrong."
Natalie Chryreva

"We make quite a team. . . . Between us, we've won 18 grand slam titles together."
Dick Enberg, on working with Evert on television

"Tennis is a lot like basketball in physical terms. And she did everything with class."
Michael Jordan, comparing himself to Evert

"Break up Chris Evert."
Curry Kirkpatrick, on Evert's dominance in tennis in the late '70s

"She came in a star and left a star."
Mike Lupica

"She kept Martina from swallowing the game whole."
Jim Murray

"She played tennis the way an orchestra plays Beethoven: deftly, lovingly, but with intense concentration on the notes."

Jim Murray

"Even if Chris had to play the match with a cast on her leg."

Jo Anne Russell, on how she would do anything to get a victory against Evert

"I think she should have a nice long honeymoon—say five years."

Jo Anne Russell, on Evert's marrying John Lloyd

"She's a great role model—for the image she projects and for the backhand. I think there must be a million kids playing who wouldn't have played if they had defensive backhands."

Ted Tinling, on Evert's two-handed backhand

"Then the handicap was Riggs's age. Here we're both old."

> *Martina Navratilova, comparing*
> *playing Jimmy Connors in an*
> *exhibition match to the Battle*
> *of the Sexes*

"It was worth the price of admission, which in my case was free."

> *Pat Sajak, on the Navratilova-*
> *Connors match*

FAMILY

"I just made spaghetti and told her not to bite her fingernails."

> *Jackie Baker, on motherly*
> *advice she gave to her daughter*
> *Mary Decker Slaney*

"I'm so focused on the game, sometimes I forget he's there until he says something in my ear."

> *Suzanne Bell, coach of a JV*
> *basketball team, on carrying her*
> *nine-month-old baby in a tote on*
> *her shoulders*

"Raffle."

> *Ruthie Bolton, member of U.S.*
> *Olympic basketball team, on the best*
> *way to distribute her four tickets*
> *among 19 brothers and sisters*

"She can hang out with the other moms—and she won't have to wear a parka."

> *Brandi Chastain, urging David*
> *Letterman to have his mother cover*
> *the U.S. women's soccer team as she*
> *did the Winter Olympics*

"There comes a time when it's probably not cool for your mom to be your best friend."

> *Lindsay Davenport, on the strained*
> *relationship between Martina Hingis*
> *and her mother*

"I guess I'm going to have to keep the gym open longer than I think."

> *Bela Karolyi, after Mary Lou Retton had a baby in 1995*

"Jackie and Florence on the same track on the same day. I wouldn't want to land that on anyone."

> *Bob Kersee, on Olympian Heike Drechsler's facing Jackie Joyner-Kersee in the long jump and sister-in-law Florence Griffith-Joyner in the 200 meters on the same day*

"She showed me her gold medals when I was a little girl. I made a bet with her that someday I'd make an Olympic team and win."

> *Kelly McCormick, silver and bronze medal winner in diving, on her gold medal winning mother, Pat*

"Just look at Reggie: he's a millionaire for being a jerk."

> *Cheryl Miller, defending her tough talking by citing the example of her brother, NBA star Reggie Miller*

"We get together for weddings, funerals, and the Olympics."

> *Kathy Murphy, cousin of Bonnie Blair, on the Blair bunch's rooting for Bonnie at the Olympics*

"I beat their mother when I was a girl in a tournament in Belgrade. Obviously, I didn't beat her badly. She managed to have three daughters after that."

> *Martina Navratilova, on beating Yulia Maleeva and her three daughters, who were all tennis pros*

"All these thoughts go through your head. I said, well, I guess I will be one of the few players that have lost to all of them."

> *Martina Navratilova, on losing at Wimbledon to one of the three Maleeva sisters, after having previously lost to the other two*

"For a long while, my son thought only women played golf."

> *Judy Rankin, on her son Walter, who spent the early part of his life on the pro tour with his mom*

"Flipped into the world."

> *Mary Lou Retton, announcing the*
> *birth of her daughter in 1995*

"Well, all that's left for me to do is go find John Lloyd and start a family."

> *Pam Shriver, after the major upsets*
> *of herself and John Lloyd in the first*
> *round of Wimbledon*

FANS

"People want to see you have a go. I reckon that's why they come out."

> *Laura Davies, on all the fans who*
> *come to watch her enormous drives*

"When I hit my drives, I hear it pretty much every hole. I never get tired of it."

> *Laura Davies, on her fans'*
> *enthusiasm*

"I like demonstrative crowds. People who pay their hard-earned money for a ticket ought to be able to make noise."

Billie Jean King

"It's like a menu: they can look, but they can't afford it."

Anna Kournikova, on all her male fans

"Sports fans in the past were predominantly men. But once people see us, they realize that athletics is changing, and so have the fans."

Rebecca Lobo

"I'm not better than them in any respect. I might play better golf than they do, but I'm nothing without them."

Nancy Lopez, on her fans

"What was I—a Martian?"

Martina Navratilova, on fans' rooting for Chris Evert and against her during a Wimbledon match

"I'm the home team everywhere."
> *Martina Navratilova, on all the fan*
> *appreciation at the end of her career*

"Unfortunately, I didn't hit balls outside the ropes, so I couldn't go out to say hello."
> *Ayako Okamato, LPGA pro, on the*
> *large number of Japanese fans*
> *cheering her at a tournament in*
> *San Diego*

FEMININITY

"If someone says it's not feminine, I say screw it."
> *Rosie Casals*

"I like to run like a man. I don't like to look like a man."
> *Florence Griffith-Joyner, on having a*
> *muscular physique yet retaining her*
> *femininity*

"I don't think being an athlete is unfeminine. I think of it as a kind of grace."
> *Jackie Joyner-Kersee*

"The big difference is I'm showered and clean when I'm modeling. The point is, I'm a woman, always."

Lisa Leslie, on being both a basketball star and a professional model

"When I'm playing, I'll sweat and talk trash. However, off the court, I'm lipstick, heels, and short skirts."

Lisa Leslie

"People accept now that a woman can be aggressive and competitive on the floor, and off the floor be a feminine woman."

Rebecca Lobo

"The one thing I wanted to do was show women that it's OK to be competitive, aggressive, and ornery and still be very feminine."

Amy Van Dyken

FENCING

"A forgiving employer."
> *Leslie Marx, on how she combines being an Olympic fencer and a business professor*

"This is a country that grew up on the gun, not the sword."
> *Carla Mae Richards, executive director of the U.S. Fencing Association, on why fencing is not popular in the United States*

LISA FERNANDEZ

"The woman's arm must have been manufactured at Lockheed."
> *Mike Downey, columnist, on the speed of the U.S. softball pitcher*

"Maybe I was the last one available."
> *Richard Callaghan, on being chosen*
> *as Nicole Bobek's eighth skating*
> *coach in eight years*

"I suppose this is a case of women's inhumanity
to men."
> *Joe Flanagan, on being fired as*
> *director of the Women's European*
> *golf tour*

"A good coach has to be willing to be fired
every day."
> *Billie Jean King*

FLAWS

"If you've got any flaws, and you're playing on the
tour, they will come up very quickly and knock
you all the way down."
> *Patty Berg, LPGA Hall of Famer*

PEGGY FLEMING

"She was poetry in motion."
Christopher Bowman

"With a lot of skaters, there's a lot of fuss and feathers, but nothing is happening. With Peggy, there's no fuss and feathers, and a great deal is happening."
Dick Button

"She can just go out and stand there and look incredible, and she will still be able to look great at 60. What she has will never go away."
Jill Trenary

FLO JO

"She was just on another level."
Evelyn Ashford, on the legendary 1988 Olympics of Florence Griffith-Joyner

"Only a man can run faster than her. Her times are phenomenal."
Evelyn Ashford

"We were dazzled by her speed, humbled by her talent, and captivated by her style."
President Bill Clinton

"She is a combination of Dennis Rodman and Michael Jordan in one."
Donna Lopiano, president, Women's Sports Foundation

"For a long time, we've been thought of as jocks. Florence brings in the glamour."
Wilma Rudolph

"If you're going to wear the outfits she does, you'd better do something in them."
Gwen Torrence, on Flo Jo's phenomenal times

FOOD FOR THOUGHT

"I'm going to eat lobsters until I'm burnt out."
Regina Jacobs, on the 5,000-meter
record she set in Maine

FRANCE

"She's about as French as an Edsel."
Bud Collins, on Mary Pierce from
Canada, who claims to be French
on the tour

"I can ski all right—if I don't have to carry France
on my back."
Carole Merle, French skier and
greatest hope for a medal in the
1992 Olympics in Lillehammer,
Norway

LINDA FRATIANNE

"She would listen and try to do exactly what she was told. If I asked her to jump off a roof, she would say, 'This roof? Or that higher roof?'"

Frank Carroll, on coaching Fratianne to a skating silver medal

FRENCH OPEN

"I'm going to enter the ladies' event maybe next year. Maybe, I'll get lucky and win that."

Pete Sampras, on having problems in the French Open

GAMBLING

"If you do well, you win loads anyway."

Laura Davies, asked as someone who loves to gamble if she ever bet on herself in a golf tournament in Great Britain (where betting on golf is legal)

"They should be bottled up inside. You want it to come out at the track."

Evelyn Ashford, on her emotions

"I know how to smile, I know how to laugh, I know how to play. But I know how to do those things only after I have finished my mission."

Nadia Comaneci, on being criticized
for not smiling during the Olympics

"They judge you on your makeup, on the way you smile, on the way you don't smile. It's very personal."

Peggy Fleming, on ice skating judges

"I am like a mussel sometimes, a closed shell. No one can get to me."

Steffi Graf

"I don't need to act mean. Not if I do what I'm capable of."

Jackie Joyner-Kersee, on suggestions
of having to act mean to do well in
the Olympics

"This is not the Ice Capades. You don't fall on a double axel and get up and smile, and everything's OK, you know."

Dottie Pepper, LPGA pro, on her grim demeanor on the tour

"I guess if looks could kill, I would have killed a number of people."

Nancy Richey, tennis great, on her intensity on the court

GLOBETROTTERS

"Where else could I be playing before 15,000 people every night?"

Nancy Lieberman, on playing for the Washington Generals, the team that always lost to the Globetrotters

"It was a dream come true. I broke the barriers. It had been an all-male party for 60 years."

Lynette Woodard, on being the first female member of the Harlem Globetrotters

GOALIES

"When I make a save, I want it to look like my grandmother can do it."

> *Briana Scurry, on her style of goaltending for the U.S. women's soccer team*

GOALS

"I want to be financially independent, stay a size six, and live to be 100."

> *Evelyn Ashford, on her life goals*

GOLD MEDAL

"A Snickers."

> *Oksana Baiul, asked what she wanted after winning the ice skating gold medal in the Olympics*

"It is because I have lived a most difficult life that I could do this."

> *Oksana Baiul, on how she was able to overcome being an orphan and physical pain to win the gold*

"It is never routine, let me tell you. Once you think it's routine, that's when it's going to be taken away from you quicker than you can think."

> *Bonnie Blair, on winning her fourth gold medal*

"I want little girls to be inspired by seeing that a women who is not like a man can win in sport. I think my medals touch all women."

> *Manuela Di Centa, glamorous Italian cross-country skier, on winning two gold medals in the '94 Olympics*

"Every time they put the silver medal around her neck, she would cry and be disgusted. She wanted the gold."

> *Natalie Granato, mother of hockey player Cammi, whose U.S. team had lost six world championships to Canada before winning the Olympic gold medal*

"When I ask myself if I want an ice cream soda, I answer, 'Not as badly as I want a gold medal.'"

Kathy Johnson, silver medal Olympic gymnast

"I cleaned my room."

Tara Lipinski, on what she did before her gold medal performance

"I guess I'll always envision this as a kind of heaven, sort of a dream world. Only this dream world was real."

Mary T. Meagher, on her three gold medals in the '84 Olympics

"I thought the best I could do was third place and now I am a winner. I think that I am dreaming."

Paraskevi Patoulidou, winner of the 100-meter hurdles in the '92 Olympics

"The gold medal outweighs the bear, most definitely."

Kim Rhode, Olympic gold medalist in shooting, whose prior highlight had been shooting a bear when she was 15

"Everybody shared in it. I never stopped smiling."
> *Dot Richardson, U.S. softball star*
> *and doctor, on showing her gold*
> *medal to all her patients*

"I just want to sit down and relax. I want to enjoy that feeling that nobody expects me to do anything great tomorrow."
> *Summer Sanders, on winning a gold*
> *medal in swimming after high*
> *expectations*

"I kissed it. I checked and I bit it. It's real."
> *Jennifer Schmidgall, member of the*
> *triumphant U.S. hockey team*

"I'd just show them my medal."
> *Briana Scurry, member of the*
> *champion U.S. soccer team, on what*
> *would have happened if she'd been*
> *stopped after fulfilling her promise to*
> *run naked in Atlanta if the team won*
> *the gold*

"No, none whatsoever."

> *Jean Shiley, 1932 U.S. gold medalist*
> *in the high jump, asked if she got*
> *any recognition for her achievement*

"I wish I could bottle the feeling I had [from winning the gold medal]; I'd be the richest person on the earth."

> *Nikki Stone, gold medal winner for*
> *aerial skiing*

"It was just the way I visualized it. I mean, wow, I've waited so long for the National Anthem to be played for me and only me."

> *Picabo Street, on winning a*
> *gold medal*

"It was like a concert and you're on stage. It was too hard to fathom that all those people were looking at you and screaming."

> *Donna Weinbrecht, on 20,000 people*
> *rooting for her to win the gold medal*
> *in freestyle skating*

"I was really flirting my way through that one."

> *Katarina Witt, on winning her second*
> *gold medal in the '88 Olympics*

"It's hard when it gets to the point where I'm hitting it so good that it gets boring."

Amy Alcott

"The best part is I've taken five strokes off my golf game."

Ellen DeGeneres, on coming out of the closet

"One week out there and you are God; next time you are the devil. But it does keep you coming back."

Juli Inkster

"It used to be that men just came out here to gape at the women. They still gape, but they also come to watch us play now."

Sally Little, on how golf has changed in the last 20 years

"I'm very relaxed when I'm playing, because it's not a job. It's a game."

Nancy Lopez

"Golf is entertainment. It has no relevance to world history."

Patty Sheehan, on those who overanalyze the importance of golf

"It's a faithless love, but you hit four good shots and you started your day right."
Dinah Shore

"I was looking for my ball in the rough, but I was hoping that the ground would swell up and suck me in."

Karen Stupples, LPGA pro, after two miserable shots in a row caused her to lose a lead in a tournament

"If the women want to play with the men, they've got to tee it up where the men tee it up."
Lee Trevino

"The old trite saying of 'One shot at a time'—it wasn't trite to me; I lived it."
Mickey Wright

GONE FISHING

"I feel great. I made enough money to go fishing."
JoAnne Carner, on finishing second
in a tour event just before her 50th
birthday

"If this year were a fish, I'd throw it back in."
Martina Navratilova, on her subpar
1988 season

EVONNE GOOLAGONG

"Evonne doesn't have to see the ball. She hits by radar."
Patti Hogan, pro tennis player

"Evonne flows. She doesn't run like the rest of us. She flows."
Bob Lansdorp, tennis coach

"In a world of Barbie dolls, Evonne is a ballerina."
Mike Lupica

"Graf's forehand is the single best stroke in the history of the game. It's the engine inside her that makes her produce big wins on the big occasions."
Mary Carillo

"Well, she's got two sides—her backhand side and suicide."
Cliff Drysdale, on Graf's phenomenal forehand

"Ninety-eight percent of the girls are scared to death to play her."
Patty Fendick

"Steffi Graf is my hero. You go hard all the time to win any match."
Jan-Michael Gambill

"A slam is amazing. I don't care if it was against old ladies or everybody was sick."
Ivan Lendl, on Graf's winning the grand slam

"Graf in an iron lung could still take most players into a three-set tiebreaker."
Jim Murray

"I think she can pretty much do anything."
Martina Navratilova

"Walking out there."
Pam Shriver, asked the turning point in a match against Graf

GREATNESS

"It's not how fast you get there; it's how long you stay."
Patty Berg

"It's a challenge for me to beat myself or do better. I try to push out of my mind not what I've accomplished but what I want to do."
Jackie Joyner-Kersee

"Seles's grunt has a lot more backswing and a better follow-through."

> *Mary Carillo, comparing the grunts of Monica Seles and Jennifer Capriati*

"If I wanted my athletes quiet, I'd go watch chess."

> *Mike Downey, on the famous grunts of Monica Seles*

"It's like someone's hitting me."

> *Monica Seles, describing her grunts*

"It sounds like she's wringing the neck of a Christmas goose."

> *Ted Tinling, on Seles's grunts*

"There is no question about her ability to race with us. She has made it in what is the most competitive racing circuit in the world."

Cale Yarborough

GYMNASTICS

"A gymnastics meet is like a hunt, in a way. It's you against them. To win, first you make your girls strong."

Bela Karolyi

"There are 10–15 gymnasts with the same technical level. Personality makes the superstar. She does everything at the right time and shocks everybody."

Bela Karolyi

"That stuff's just for show, to make us look classier than we really are."

Mary Lou Retton, on the practice of gymnasts tiptoeing on the stage

"He was setting the pace. I wasn't about to run away from the president."

> *Rebecca Lobo, on running with*
> *President Clinton*

"I wouldn't call that wimpy, but on the other hand, you don't exactly get an aerobic workout."

> *Pam Shriver, on President Bush and*
> *his love of horseshoes*

"Bill's actually quite handsome for someone his age."

> *Picabo Street, on meeting then*
> *46-year-old President Clinton*

"I don't know. I've never talked to a president before."

> *Kerri Strug, on what it was like to*
> *receive a congratulatory call from*
> *President Clinton*

"The president was really cool. He's really casual and laid back."

> *Jenny Thompson, Olympic swimmer, on meeting President Clinton at an Olympic rally*

HAIRCUT

"I like your Dorothy Hamill haircut."

> *Tour guide, giving a museum tour to Dorothy Hamill and not recognizing her*

HALL OF FAME

"My headstone will read, 'Here lies Amy Alcott, winner of 29 tour titles but not a member of the Hall of Fame.'"

> *Amy Alcott, prior to changing of the rule that permitted entry to the LPGA Hall of Fame only after 30 tournament wins*

"In a way, it feels weird. I never felt like I retired."

Tracy Austin, on being the youngest inductee to the Tennis Hall of Fame at age 29

"You need 30 wins to qualify for the Hall of Fame. It's important to me. Besides, it makes a great obituary."

JoAnne Carner, on qualifying for the LPGA Hall of Fame

"If you're going to do that, let's don't call it the Hall of Fame; let's call it the Make Everybody Happy Club."

Mickey Wright, on plans to lower the standards for entry into the LPGA Hall of Fame

DOROTHY HAMILL

"Perfection."

Dick Button, on Hamill's performance in the '76 Olympics

"What a time to Hamm it up."
> Chicago Tribune *headline, after the*
> *United States defeated Denmark in*
> *the soccer World Cup*

"When Mia is playing her best, there's no one better in the world."
> *Tony DiCicco, U.S. World Cup*
> *soccer coach*

"She has that Michael Jordan impact. She gets the ball, and everybody holds their breath. You might get to see something you've never seen before."
> *Anson Dorrance, coach of the U.S.*
> *women's World Cup team in the*
> *mid-'80s*

"Mia has that amazing ability to go right through defenders—as if by molecular displacement."
> *Anson Dorrance*

"Simply the greatest women's player of all time. You cannot say that too many times."
> *Phil Knight, CEO of Nike*

"We did our best to track her down. But, unfortunately, she was not tracked down."

Ismaila Mabo, Nigerian soccer coach, on trying to contain Hamm during the World Cup

"One time they wanted to be like Mike. Now they want to be like Mia."

Dean Stoyer, Nike ad director

TONYA HARDING

"Look up *dysfunctional* in the dictionary and you'll see her spring and triple axel next to it."

David Hans Schmidt, Harding's agent

"When I would go back to school, I could see all my friends had grown over the summer. But they only did that once. Me, I kept growing."

Margo Dydek, 7'2" center in
the WNBA

"Size doesn't matter as long as you can get to the end of the pool faster than everybody else."

Janet Evans, on being 5'1"

"I want all of you kids to focus on just one thing: grow taller."

Debbie Leonard, former Duke
University basketball coach,
advising her team

"That's why I'm so doggone short. He keeps patting me on the top of the head whenever I do something right."

Mary Lou Retton, on her coach,
Bela Karolyi

"Small as I am, every time I shot the ball, they smacked it in my face, and a fast break was going the other way."

Dawn Staley, on how she was forced into being such a good passer

CAROL HEISS

"I like Carol Heiss very much as a sportswoman. . . . As a girl? Of course I am in love with her. Isn't everybody?"

Evgeni Grishin, Soviet Olympian

HEPTATHLON

"I like the heptathlon because it shows you what you're made of."

Jackie Joyner-Kersee

"Martina is the most thoughtful woman I have ever seen on the court. She has great anticipation and a real sense of the game."
Bud Collins

"This kid is simply smarter than everybody else."
Andrea Leand

"Martina beats you with court savvy and high-percentage tennis. She's the best all-court player I've ever seen."
Pam Shriver

"She was born to play tennis. You cannot work at this. Even if you worked at it, you cannot have it like she has."
Irina Spirlea

HISTORY

"It happened like 2,000 years ago and has nothing to do with what I have to do now."

Jennifer Capriati, on history

"That little dead dude."

Jennifer Capriati, early in her career, on Napoleon Bonaparte

HOBBIES

"Yeah, dolls."

Babe Didrikson, asked if there was ever anything she didn't play

"I really don't think of it as that [important]. I just think of it as signing a card and making the team."

Rachel Barrie, age 15, on being the first girl to play junior hockey in Canada

"For so many years, people told you that you shouldn't be on the ice because it was women's hockey and you couldn't go anywhere, and here you are with a gold medal around your neck."

Cammi Granato, on the United States's winning the hockey gold medal in the '96 Olympics

"As much as I love hockey, there's more to life than sitting in the stands trying to avoid being hit by a puck."

Janet Jones, actress and wife of Wayne Gretzky

"They're much, much better looking."
> *David Letterman, on having the U.S.*
> *women's hockey team come to the*
> *studio instead of the men's*

"I had a feeling of joy go through my body when I saw an Olympic gold medal being hung around the neck of a female hockey player."
> *Shannon Miller, coach of the*
> *Canadian hockey team that lost*
> *to the United States in the gold*
> *medal game*

"You felt so good for them, the way they were just bleeding for each other to win every game."
> *Mike Richter, U.S. hockey goalie,*
> *on the U.S. women's Olympic*
> *hockey team*

"Our team had no idols. Now teams to come will have us."
> *Angela Ruggiero*

"The only thing I like more than hockey is women's hockey."
> *Susan Sarandon*

"Growing up, I had to play on boys' hockey teams. Maybe now boys will want to play on mine."

Jennifer Schmidgall, member of the U.S. Olympic hockey team

"I thought it would be the 'Blue Danube Waltz,' really."

Ben Smith, coach of the U.S. Olympic hockey team, on the feistiness of a game with no stakes between Canada and the United States prior to the gold medal game

"The whole concept that hockey is a running game has come hard on Canada. In Canada, either you skate or you walk. Hockey is a running sport, so you train virtually as if for track."

Marina van der Merwe, former Canadian women's hockey coach, on training her team to run

"The first left winger I ever had a crush on."

Barry Wilbon, Washington Post reporter, on the women's Olympic hockey team's A. J. Mleczko

"She's it. She's definitely the future of women's basketball."

Teresa Edwards

"Meek is fun to watch—exciting with a lot of skills. She'll definitely take women's sports to a new high."

Michael Jordan

"The mark of a great player is, can you score zero points and still make a difference? Chamique can do that."

Ann Meyers

"Spring break."

Pat Summitt, Tennessee basketball coach, asked before the NCAA finals where Tennessee would have been without Holdsclaw

HORSE RACING

"If you try to run with her, you won't stay the distance; if you don't run with her, you'll never catch her. Either way, you're dead."

Wayne Lukas, trainer of the female winner of the 1988 Kentucky Derby, Winning Colors

HORSING AROUND

"The rest of it is wasted time."

Julie Krone, champion jockey, on what she does when she is not around horses

HURRAY FOR HOLLYWOOD

"I'd rather gulp poison than try my hand at motion pictures."

Ethel Catherwood, 1928 Olympic gold medal winner in the high jump, on offers from Hollywood

"I'm looking forward to doing movies with big actors because it will be a big lesson for me."

Pasha Grishuk, Russian gold medalist in ice dancing, on her future ambitions

"They paid me $450 a week, and they sent me to school to lose my Brooklyn accent."

Eleanor Holm, Olympic swimmer, on her acting career in the 1930s

"I'd love to do some movies. I am the next Rambette."

Cheryl Miller, on future ambitions

"I'll just act."

Monica Seles, on her goal to be an entertainer even though she can't sing

"From my movies, people realized that women wouldn't die from chlorine. Women could be athletic and attractive—and they wouldn't catch cold from having a wet head."

Esther Williams

"I've signed Miss Henie and her skates. Even if she couldn't skate, I'd have signed her anyway, but not for so much money."

Darryl Zanuck, on the star power of Sonja Henie

FLO HYMAN

"She strikes the ball with enough ferocity to rearrange the grain in a wood floor."

Joan Ackerman Blount, on Hyman's prowess on the volleyball court

ICE DANCING

"Then you find out that they're really brother and sister. And you go, 'Oooh. Get me out of here.'"

Garry Shandling, on ice dancers who look so romantic together

ICE SKATING

"Most of the great female skaters I have known, like Dorothy Hamill or Peggy Fleming or Linda Fratianne, always appeared frail on the outside. But all of them were the opposite. They all had inner cores of metal and steel."

> *Frank Carroll, ice skating coach*

"I always tell my girls, 'Think like a man, but act and look like a woman.'"

> *Carol Heiss, gold medalist and ice skating coach*

"The jumps were never supposed to mean so much. . . . You need the caressing of the ice."

> *Carol Heiss*

"Ours is not simply a sport, but also an art. It combines beauty and athletics."

> *Sonja Henie*

"It's just the nature of the sex. The boys can go out there and turn their emotions off. They don't get so rattled, not as much as the girls do. If the girls can learn to do that from the guys, they can probably beat the guys."

> *Dody Teachman, former trainer of*
> *Tonya Harding*

ICE WARS
(KERRIGAN—HARDING)

"I was going to sue her for defamation of character, but then I realized I have no character."

> *Charles Barkley, on Tonya Harding's*
> *calling herself the Charles Barkley*
> *of skating*

"Nancy and Sluggo."

> Boston Herald *headline, before the*
> *Olympic confrontation of Nancy*
> *Kerrigan and Tonya Harding*

"Maybe our students had better take martial arts and figure skating at the same time."

> *Frank Carroll, Michelle Kwan's*
> *coach, on Tonya Harding*

"I'm going to start selling hot chocolate and coffee."

> *Karen Courtland, U.S. skater, on the more than 500 reporters covering Kerrigan and Harding during practice*

"You know that every once in a while, someone might strike it rich in figure skating. It's too bad this time it took a bang on the knee to do it."

> *Claire Ferguson, president of the U.S. Figure Skating Association, on the millions of dollars likely to be made by Nancy Kerrigan*

"Amy Fisher on skates."

> *Tony Kornheiser, columnist, on Tonya Harding*

"In the post-Tonya era, figure skating has become disfigure skating."

> *Tony Kornheiser*

"CBS had so much success with last week's "Nancy Kerrigan and Friends,' they're coming back next week with another special, 'Tonya Harding and Accomplices.'"

David Letterman

"After last year, this is rather small potatoes, wouldn't you say?"

John Nicks, skating coach, on the "party girl" reputation of ice-skater Nicole Bobek

"Safer."

Kristi Yamaguchi, on how she felt about not seeking a second gold medal in 1994 during the Kerrigan-Harding era

IDITAROD

"I don't think anyone who is a true pioneer thinks of themselves as one. They're just doing something they have a passion for."

Susan Butcher, four-time winner of the Iditarod

"Twelve or thirteen, I forget."
>
> *Michelle Akers, soccer star, on her*
> *number of knee surgeries*

"A physique that seemed to have dealt more with wrecking balls than tennis balls."
>
> *Bud Collins, on the injury-plagued*
> *Andrea Jaeger*

"We all thought old Cindy was immortal."
>
> *Christian Cooper, on an injury*
> *suffered by 28-year-old Olympic skier*
> *Cindy Nelson*

"I dream about being healthy. That's all I need to be."
>
> *Mary Decker, on her ambitions*

"I'm not going to allow you to do this. This isn't a coach-athlete thing. This is your husband talking."
>
> *Bob Kersee, on Jackie Joyner-Kersee's*
> *dropping out of the heptathlon*
> *because of severe pain*

"I've got a 16-year-old mind—but I feel like a 60-year-old body."

> *Iva Majoli, 16-year-old tennis player, on her many injuries*

"I met my old friend, Mr. Speed, and I was flying again."

> *Picabo Street, on recovering from an injury*

"I could feel it slipping away. I felt like I had to do it."

> *Kerri Strug, on her Olympic vault in which she jumped with torn ligaments*

INSPIRATION

"Our greatness and vibrancy is born out of having a dream and going for it alone if necessary. It is about ceaselessly striving for excellence and achieving it."

> *Michelle Akers, on the inspiration of the U.S. soccer team*

"Really bad disco."

> *Heather Fuhr, triathlete, on what*
> *inspires her during a triathlon*

"While I'm lying there, my competition is out there getting better. That motivates me."

> *Marion Jones, runner, on why she is*
> *rarely not practicing*

"I didn't want to cop out on my own potential."

> *Diann Roffe-Steinrotter, U.S. gold*
> *medalist in the super giant slalom*

"*I can't* are two words that have never been in my vocabulary. I believe in me more than anything in the world."

> *Wilma Rudolph*

INSURANCE

"They wanted an arm and a leg."

> *Martina Navratilova, on why she*
> *didn't insure her left arm*

IRELAND

"How many people are in Ireland?"
> *Sonia O'Sullivan, on winning the*
> *gold medal in the 1995 World*
> *Championship—40,000 people had*
> *come to greet her at the airport*
> *after she won the silver in the*
> *'93 World Championship*

"I have a message for Ireland: Don't drink too much before I come home—save some for me."
> *Michelle Smith, after winning*
> *three gold medals in the Olympics*
> *and being told of celebrations all*
> *over Ireland*

ANDREA JAEGER

"She plays like she's double-parked."
> *Mary Carillo, on Jaeger's*
> *impatient style*

JEWELRY

"I'm going to play the 14th hole 54 times. That's the only hole I want to play."

> *Terry-Jo Myers, LPGA pro, on an event where anyone who gets a hole in one on the 14th hole wins a $1 million mother-of-pearl necklace*

JOBS

"You've got to have fun. Otherwise, this would be too much like a real job."

> *Laura Davies, on not spending a lot of time on practice*

"This is me, doing what I want to do and getting paid for it. It's just sick."

> *Picabo Street, on her career as a skier*

JOCKEYS

"I ride because I love horses."
Mary Bacon, on the impact of her being one of the first female jockeys

MARION JONES

"You don't put limits on what Marion Jones can do. In anything. Period."
Dennis Craddock, former coach

"Marion Jones is the answer to the 'track is dead' talk."
Jon Drummond, sprinter

"I don't know what she can't do."
Jackie Joyner-Kersee

"Marion Jones has world records in her legs."
Louise Mead Tricard, track historian

"She was one in a million. She was like Michael Jordan. You just couldn't beat her."
Cindy Greiner, former heptathlete

"You have proved to the world that you are the greatest athlete who ever lived, male or female."
Bruce Jenner

"I always cheer for my athlete, never for my wife."
Bob Kersee, on difficulties of coaching his wife

"Anybody who can put it all together as she has is absolutely phenomenal."
Bob Mathias, decathlon gold medalist

"It was such an honor to train with Jackie. I mean she's unbelievable. Her body is unbelievable."
Monica Seles

"There's no argument that she is the greatest female athlete of all time."
Dwight Stones

"Those calling her America's greatest athlete since Jim Thorpe might not be exaggerating."
David Woods, columnist

JUDO

"It's not so much trouble throwing them—it's watching that you don't land underneath them."
Colleen Rosensteel, U.S. Olympic judo heavyweight, on 300-pound opponents

KIDS

"By the 2002 Olympics, the persons watching Leno will be in rest homes. Picabo talked to the kids. They'll be the mainstream."
Stubby Street, Picabo's father, on her impact on young children

KILL THE UMP

"Are you late for tea?"

> *Kathy Horvath, after losing a match*
> *point in Wimbledon on a bad call by*
> *the umpire*

BILLIE JEAN KING

"Billie Jean was Joan of Arc in a miniskirt."
> *Bud Collins*

"No man or woman in tennis has made such an
extraordinary triple threat as Billie Jean in
advancing herself, women, and the game as a
whole."
> *Bud Collins*

"She put money in my pocket and the pockets of
all women tennis players."
> *Chris Evert*

"You know all that sports psychology stuff? Well, she invented that."
  Mary Carillo

"On the court, she's an evil, merciless bastard. Totally ruthless. She'll do everything and anything within the rules to win."
  Frank Hammond, professional referee

"No one changes the world who isn't obsessed."
  Billie Jean King

"She was so crazy about tennis, I'd have to lock her in her room to do her homework."
  Alice Marble, King's coach

"I think the women should give Billie Jean 5½ percent of every paycheck they get."
  John McEnroe

"Billie Jean at her best was the greatest, from what I saw. If we played, I don't know that I could pick a winner, but I'd love to play her in her prime."
  Martina Navratilova

"Records are made to be broken. If mine has to go, I would like Billie Jean to have it, because she has so much guts."

Elizabeth Ryan, on King's beating her record of 20 Wimbledon titles

"If she didn't have a platform, she'd wither."
Ted Tinling

"Today's young women athletes don't have a clue they're where they are because of the courage of Billie Jean King."

Willye White, former Olympian

KLUTZ

"I will never understand how she can ski down a mountain at 50 or 60 miles an hour, then come home and fall down the stairs."

Heather Percy, on her daughter Karen, a bronze medalist in the women's downhill and the family klutz

"A wild colt. I've given up trying to rein her in. The girl's a goddamn Dennis Rodman."
Vic Braden

"She loves the spotlight. Her attitude toward everybody else is 'peel me a grape.'"
Mary Carillo

"The Princess of Tabloids."
Bud Collins

"She's very pretty, but I'm sure she'd like to change places with me. Everyone is making ours out to be a rivalry, but so far it hasn't been."
Martina Hingis, on consistently beating Kournikova

"I can certainly remember a change happening, when you had big outfits (companies), and the nice horses, and the people who would take a chance on a girl—it wasn't an oddity."

Diane Nelson, jockey, on Krone's impact on horse racing

"She's not just a great women jockey, she's a great jockey."

Gary Stevens

"I don't think of Julie as a girl; I think of her as a rider—a great rider. She has courage that cannot be measured."

Nick Zito, horse trainer

MICHELLE KWAN

"When all those 6.0s came up, I thought, 'Am I hearing this right?'"

> *Michelle Kwan, on getting perfect scores from all seven judges during the U.S. skating championships*

"She puts her heart and soul out there with incredibly beautiful movements."

> *Katarina Witt*

LABOR DEPARTMENT

"No marathon has ever been as difficult as labor."

> *Joan Benoit Samuelson*

"He knew he was going to have to wait. He figured it might as well be at the rink."

> *Bonnie Blair, sixth child in her family, on her dad's dropping her mom off in the hospital in labor and going over to the rink to practice*

"The all-verb final."

> *Mary Carillo, on Sabine Hack*
> *and Mary Pierce playing in a*
> *tournament final*

"I was trying to add a little color. Unfortunately, what I added was off-color."

> *Lori Garbacz, LPGA pro, on being*
> *fined for shouting an obscenity on*
> *the course*

"*Good shot, bad luck,* and *hell* are the five basic words to be used in a game of tennis, though those, of course, can be slightly amplified."

> *Virginia Graham*

"I can't swear as quickly in German."

> *Melanie Molitor, mother and coach*
> *of Martina Hingis, on why she*
> *speaks Czech to Martina*

"David Stern and I talked about it. We're not letting Dennis play in both leagues."

Val Ackerman, commissioner of the WNBA, on the cross-dressing of Dennis Rodman

"I was afraid she wouldn't behave herself, but she did."

Annabelle Lee, former member of the All-American Girls Professional Baseball League, on the casting of Madonna in the movie A League of Their Own

LEGACY

"Someday they may look back at me as the grandma of freestyle."

Donna Weinbrecht, gold medalist in freestyle skiing, on her legacy

LEGENDS

"I've always wanted to be a legend, and to be known, not because of a gold medal, but just because of my skating."

> *Michelle Kwan, on her decision not to turn pro*

"Men hand their heroes to their sons. Little boys know about Mickey Mantle and Jackie Robinson and never saw them play. Women have to do the same thing."

> *Nancy Lieberman*

SUZANNE LENGLEN

"Suzanne is the finest of all champions, for she wins and wins and still avoids the reproach of being an idea of a good example to anyone."

> *Heywood Broun, on the lifestyle of the tennis great*

LISA LESLIE

"Whether I'm on the court or the runway, I'm out there entertaining. They're the same for me."
Lisa Leslie, on her careers in the
WNBA and as a model

"Lisa's dominating and physical, and then, after the game is over, she transforms into this stunning woman."
James Worthy, former NBA player

NANCY LIEBERMAN

"She's not a woman out there; she's a player."
Nate "Tiny" Archibald, NBA Hall of
Famer, on playing in a summer
league with Lieberman

"She's always been a pugnacious SOB, but she doesn't have the speed or strength to compete with the men."

Al Lewis, actor and former basketball
team owner

LIFE WISDOM

"It's better to look ahead and prepare than to look back and regret."
Jackie Joyner-Kersee

TARA LIPINSKI

"She's not a child and she's not a woman, but *teenager* isn't a good enough word for her."
Sandra Bezic, skating commentator

"I can't physically remove her."
Richard Callaghan, Lipinski's coach, on how much she loves to practice

"Lipinski has said she gave up amateur competition so that she could spend more time with her family, making her perhaps the only teenager in America who actually wants to live at home."
Alice Park, Time

"You have a gold medal but no driver's license."
*Oprah Winfrey, on Lipinski's winning
a gold medal at age 15*

LITTLE MO

"I was a strange little girl armed with hate, fear,
and a Golden Racket."
Maureen Connolly

"She didn't just beat you—she dispatched you."
Ted Tinling

REBECCA LOBO

"I can't say any one thing. But the sum of all the
parts is unreal."
*Geno Auriemma, University of
Connecticut coach, on the greatness
of Lobo*

LOCKER ROOM

"I don't think my wife likes it. It would make me uncomfortable if my wife were naked in a locker room and men were reporting in there."

> *Howie Long, on female reporters in locker rooms*

"What I say to people who gripe about women in the locker room is just two words—male gynecologists."

> *Julie Vader, sports reporter in Oregon*

"I don't care about women's rights: I'm not having a woman in my locker room."

> *Bill Yeoman, college football coach, who would not let any women into the locker room after the Cotton Bowl*

LONG JUMP

"They'd see me long-jump and say, 'Why is Jackie always falling?'"

> *Jackie Joyner-Kersee, on her nieces'*
> *watching her long-jump on TV*

LOOKS COULD KILL

"'You're an athlete? Funny, you don't look like an athlete.' Well, what is an athlete supposed to look like?"

> *Estelle Baskerville, high jumper in*
> *the '68 Olympics, on what boys tell*
> *her on dates*

"Being pretty, ugly, or semi has no effect on the golf ball. It doesn't help your score if you're pretty."

> *Laura Baugh, attractive player on*
> *the LPGA tour*

"You couldn't afford me, boys."

*Anna Kournikova, on boys whistling
at her at tennis matches*

"It's human nature for people to notice [me]. If I
had plastic surgery to make me look worse, maybe
that would help."

Anna Kournikova

"In the world of Wayne and Garth, if she were a
president, she'd be Babe-raham Lincoln."

*Dan Shaughnessy, columnist, on Uta
Pippig, winner of the Boston
Marathon*

"It was good for the game of golf. But it wasn't
good for my golf game."

*Jan Stephenson, on being the former
pinup girl of the LPGA*

NANCY LOPEZ

"Nancy with the smiling face."

*Dave Anderson, on the always
friendly and personable Lopez*

"People who have never played golf in their life, they know her name. That's a very rare thing."
JoAnne Carner

"She plays by feel. All her senses come into play. That's when golf is an art."
Carol Mann

TEGLA LOROUPE

"You know she's awesome when you have more Americans cheering for her than we did."
Shelly Steely, on the winning performance of Loroupe, who is from Kenya, in the 10,000 at the Goodwill Games held in the United States

LOSING

"Sometimes I think it's me, that I can't finish out the match. Then I realize most of it's Martina."
Chris Evert, on losing 13 times in a row to Martina Navratilova

"I think the whole game hinged on one call—the one I made last April scheduling the game."

Peter Gavitt, women's basketball coach at Maine, after his team lost 115–57

"Things got so bad that I had to play my student manager for a while. Things got really bad when she started to complain to the press that she wasn't getting enough playing time."

Linda Hill-McDonald, Minnesota basketball coach, after a 6–22 season

"Failure is feedback."

Billie Jean King

"It's hard to promote a funeral."

Frank Layden, coach of the Utah Starzz of the WNBA, on their record of 8–22

"We didn't get our kids prepared the first five minutes."

Tricia Sacca, Quinnipiac coach, on losing a game 117–20

"I go out each match thinking I'm going to lose, so it doesn't make a difference to me."

Monica Seles

LUGE

"I've always needed to stick out—to be noticed and feel accepted. Luge does that. I'm finally somebody."

Bonnie Warner, U.S. Olympian
in luge

MALAPROPS AND FRACTURED SYNTAX

"Only bothers me when I sleep because I can't sleep."

Carling Bassett, tennis pro, on
her cough

"Training has to be everything, but not too much."

Kim Gallagher, track star

"It's fine. I cough a lot more than I ever have."
Kim Gallagher, on the pollution in
Los Angeles before the Olympics

"The mayor of Michigan."
Tara Lipinski, on who called to
congratulate her after she won the
gold medal

"I can only think of two words to say—thanks."
Pat McCormick, diving champion,
after receiving an award

"This game is 80 percent mental, and if you can conquer it mentally, you've got half of it beat."
Betty Richardson, amateur golfer

"Win or lose, I want people to know that 115 percent went into my effort."
Amy Van Dyken

HANA MANDLIKOVA

"Hana can beat any player on any given day, unless Hana is playing on the same given day."
Carling Bassett

"Hana went in under the Czech flag, and I've had a checkered career."
Bud Collins, on why it was appropriate that he and Mandlikova entered the Hall of Fame at the same time

MARATHONS

"The one thing I'll tell my grandchildren is that one time I ran alone on the L.A. freeway."
Joan Benoit Samuelson, on winning the Olympic marathon in Los Angeles

"A maternithon for expectant mothers."
Bud Collins, on Joan Benoit Samuelson's running in the Boston Marathon while pregnant

"This marathon will be like my marriage—my first and last."

> *Gwyn Coogan, running her first*
> *marathon in the '92 Olympics*

"Running a marathon is much easier than having a baby."

> *Miki Gorman, marathoner*

"I have the dream of running the marathon because I just love running."

> *Florence Griffith-Joyner, on her plans*
> *to compete in the '96 Olympics*

"Women will throw away their spiked heels and pick up jogging shoes in record numbers."

> *Fred LeBow, race promoter, on Joan*
> *Benoit Samuelson's winning the gold*
> *medal in the marathon*

"If you only learn how to run by your mistakes, you'll be running marathons until you're 150 before you get it right."

> *Lisa Martin, Olympic silver medalist*
> *in the marathon*

"When I was first running marathons, we were sailing on a flat earth. We were afraid we'd get big legs, grow mustaches, not get boyfriends, not be able to have babies."

Katherine Switzer, on being the first woman in the Boston Marathon in 1967

MARRIAGE

"It's a Greek tragedy. I'm getting the work I want, and I'm inflicting pain on myself by being away so much."

Mary Carillo, on how her travel schedule as an announcer affects her marriage

"We get along so well because I eventually get my way."

Bob Kersee, on his relationship with his wife, Jackie Joyner-Kersee

"It's 40–love one minute and love–40 the next."

Billie Jean King, on how marriage is like tennis

"It's good to be wise as a woman. You never know who will marry you and want you to stay at home. If you have property, they will respect you."

> *Tegla Loroupe, Kenyan marathoner, on why it was important for her to win money*

"We're not saying our vows in water, and we're not swimming off in the ocean afterwards."

> *Summer Sanders, gold medal swimmer, announcing her wedding plans*

"I feel so used. Now that the wedding's over, she doesn't need me anymore."

> *Michael Smith, ex-husband of Tonya Harding*

CHRISTY MARTIN

"Tenacious and vivacious."

> *Don King, describing Martin's championship boxing style*

"She's awesome. She could beat half the lightweights out there. She's definitely king of the women."

Jimmy Maloney, Martin's sparring partner

MEDIA FRENZY

"Media coverage of women's sports seems to concentrate more on sex rather than skill."

Tony Banks, British sports minister, on the coverage of women at Wimbledon

"I hope people would report me for how hard I tried at these Olympics and not how I did."

Nicole Bobek, U.S. skater, on finishing 17th in the '98 Olympics

"We talked about the silly questions we get asked by the media."

Nancy Kerrigan, asked what she and roommate Kristi Yamaguchi talked about during the '92 Olympics

"Sometimes I just want to stand in front of everybody and say, 'Hey, leave her alone.'"

> *Nancy Lopez, on the media pressure surrounding Se Ri Pak*

"In Czechoslovakia, there is no such thing as freedom of the press. In the United States, there is no such thing as freedom from the press."

> *Martina Navratilova*

"I don't mind a lie here and there, but it should at least be realistic."

> *Martina Navratilova, on the British tabloids*

"Little girls who watch the WNBA can see that if they don't want to play the game, they can always grow up to cover it."

> *Lisa Olsen, sports reporter*

"Being a sportscaster was my way of becoming a professional athlete."

> *Robin Roberts, on the limited athletic options available to her*

"**I** put the broad in broadcasting."

> *Sherry Ross, the first female*
> *professional hockey announcer*

"**W**hy should I? I already know what the truth is about me."

> *Summer Sanders, on never reading*
> *anything about herself*

"**I**t's frustrating to see the attention she gets. I just want to shut [the media's] mouth."

> *Irina Spirlea, on all the attention*
> *heaped on Anna Kournikova*

"**W**hat people read about you in today's paper, they will use tomorrow to take out old flowers."

> *Grete Waitz, legendary*
> *distance runner*

MEDIA WATCH

"**I** don't want to be graded on a curve."

> *Mary Carillo, on being called the*
> *best women's tennis expert*

"When I was a kid, all I wanted to do was play tennis and watch TV. Now all I want to do is watch tennis and play TV."

Mary Carillo

"That would be great. We could exchange gunfire in the booth."

Mary Carillo, on sharing the announcing booth with John McEnroe

"The people who hired me weren't interested in my perspective as a woman; they were looking for my perspective as a golfer."

Judy Rankin, on covering the U.S. Men's Open

"I wasn't at the dawn of women covering sports, but I made the breakfast."

Lesley Visser, on being a pioneer as a female sports reporter

MEDIOCRITY

"My volley is blah. I'm a dead elephant on the court. My serve has no sting, and I am confused. Other than that, I'm a fine player."

Mona Schallau, touring tennis pro

MENTAL GAME

"The trouble with me is I think too much. I always said you have to be dumb to play golf."

JoAnne Carner

"Once you think about it, though, it's gone."

Beth Daniels, on tying the record of nine birdies in a row but being unable to break it

"It's good to be really experienced or really naive."

Janet Evans, on her Olympic experiences

"I don't think I have any. I just throw dignity to the winds and think of nothing but the game."

Suzanne Lenglen, 1919 Wimbledon champion, on her methods of play

"I just try to concentrate on concentrating."

Martina Navratilova, on the key to her success

"It takes a very special person to be mentally tough for nine seconds."

Wilma Rudolph, on being a star of the 100-yard dash

"As soon as I get into tactics, I get into trouble."
Monica Seles

"I just play."

Patty Sheehan, LPGA golfer, on the technical aspects of the game she thinks of during a tournament

"The golf demons always play havoc with my brain at night."

Patty Sheehan

MILITARY

"Wouldn't you want me on the front lines?"
Martina Navratilova, on the
controversy about gays in
the military

CHERYL MILLER

"I could be All-Pro five times and Most Valuable
Player twice and I'd still be known as Cheryl
Miller's brother."
Reggie Miller, NBA star

SHANNON MILLER

"She's a shy teenager in real life. But when she
steps onto the floor, she's an actress."
Peggy Liddick, gymnastics
choreographer

MISS AMERICA

"I'm a normal woman. I've dated a lot of guys.
I've had a few drinks. I've told dirty jokes. I've
cursed. I've been rude to my parents. I'm a
normal person."

Chris Evert, on her clean image

MIXED DOUBLES

"Talk to any marriage counselor and you'll learn
that mixed doubles have caused more divorces
than mothers-in-law."

Bud Collins

"When Billie wanted a ball, I moved out of the
way. Nobody ever intimidated her."

*Owen Davidson, Billie Jean King's
mixed doubles partner*

"I'm playing mixed doubles next year, but I should give someone else a chance to win an event."

Martina Hingis, on winning both the singles and doubles at the Australian Open

"No, not really, but I guess I've never seen it any other way."

Billie Jean King, on not realizing that they had a full crowd for a mixed doubles match at center court in Wimbledon, a rare occurrence

"Mixed was always my favorite, ahead of singles. There was nothing like testing yourself against the hardest-hitting guys."

Billie Jean King

"Hit at the girl whenever possible."

Bill Tilden, on his advice for playing mixed doubles

"He's going to take the trophy, and I'm going to take the check."

Serena Williams, on winning $120,000 and a trophy with her mixed doubles partner Max Mirnyi

"Rae's happy about the money but sad about the time. I'm sad about the money but happy about my time."

> *Janet Bowie, after finishing first in a race but because of her amateur status being ineligible for the $1,000 check which went to second-place finisher Rae Stiger*

"I cannot find a job that pays me $700,000 a year, so until I do, I'll be right here."

> *Pat Bradley, asked if she planned on retiring from the LPGA*

"Sometimes a shorter opera is much better than a long one."

> *Bud Collins, defending women's tennis from critics who claim men should get more because their matches are longer*

"I like to make presents to myself a lot."

Martina Hingis, on what she
would do with a $10 million
endorsement deal

"The best thing about the revolution is now I get to keep the money."

Doina Melinte, Romanian runner

"I like the thought of playing for money instead of silverware. I never did like to polish."

Patty Sheehan, on turning pro

"Here it's about who ends up with the most money."

Samantha Tomlanson, Australian
basketball star, on life in the
United States

"This is a check for $24,000, but for me it's just a piece of paper."

Natasha Zvereva, Soviet tennis star,
on winning a tournament before the
changes in the Soviet Union

"I won 50 tournaments and won a little under $200,000. She has won over five million. If that wouldn't make you want to toss your cookies, I don't know what would."

Louise Suggs, tongue-in-cheek introduction of Beth Daniels at her LPGA Hall of Fame induction

MOTHER RUSSIA

"In my soul, I've always been a Russian."

Elena Valbe, gold medal winning member of the Unified Team after the demise of the Soviet Union

MOTIVATION

"When you're in a sport like speed skating, when the clock gives you the result, there is always a faster goal or a personal best to beat."

Bonnie Blair, on what motivates her

"That's not pressure; that's incentive."

> *Francie Larrieu Smith, on her*
> *husband's making the Olympic*
> *team in the 200*

"They say, 'go home, have babies, wash dishes. . . .'
When people said those things, it also made me
stronger."

> *Rosa Mota, Olympic champion*
> *marathoner from Portugal, on how*
> *she was motivated at an early age*

"She holds on to the positive things, but if someone
says something that's not too nice, she holds on to
that, and it really motivates her."

> *Mark Schubert, coach of Janet Evans*

MURALS

"It's overwhelming. Every time I go by there, it just
seems like it gets bigger. It's too big for me."

> *Dawn Staley, U.S. Olympic*
> *basketball team member, on the*
> *huge mural of her in Philadelphia*

NATIONAL ANTHEM

"I thought I'd like to hear the National Anthem."
> *Lindsay Davenport, on her*
> *motivation for winning the gold*
> *medal in the '96 Olympics*

"I kept forgetting the middle part. I would juggle around the ramparts and rockets' red glare. But I think I nailed it tonight."
> *Picabo Street, on singing the*
> *National Anthem after winning*
> *the gold medal*

MARTINA NAVRATILOVA

"She's like the old Green Bay Packers: you know exactly what she's going to do, but there isn't a thing you can do about it."
> *Arthur Ashe*

"How to shake hands."

> *Bettina Bunge, on what she learned*
> *from losing to Navratilova 11 times*
> *in a row*

"She dared to be great. She dared to play her game. She dared to live her life the way she wanted."

> *Bud Collins*

"Martina is the best athlete I've seen in tennis and probably the best ever."

> *Chris Evert*

"Why don't you just join the men's tour circuit and leave us alone."

> *Chris Evert, after being dominated by*
> *Navratilova in a match*

"Kick her in the shins."

> *Evonne Goolagong, on the best way*
> *to beat her*

"When I beat her at Wimbledon, it was like winning a grand slam."

> *Jana Novotna*

"She was beside herself—which, come to think of it, would make a great doubles team."

> Scott Ostler, columnist, on
> Navratilova's throwing a
> temper tantrum

"She goes from arrogance to panic with nothing in between."

> Ted Tinling

"She seems a freak of nature, the perfect tennis player."

> Virginia Wade

NERVES

"I look at the tapes: I look calm as anything. Inside I was just going, Aughh! Get me out of here."

> Peggy Fleming

"I don't throw up."

> Sandra Haynie, on the difference in
> her game over the last 20 years

"I take long walks at night through the cemetery. It calms me down."

> *Cho Youn Jeong, gold medal archer, on how she calms down before a major event*

"You can't win an Olympic championship by being nervous. I don't want a wimp out there. You skated like a jelly bean."

> *Alex McGowan, coach to skater Debi Thomas after a bad practice routine*

"No, I didn't have nerves. Not nervous."

> *Se Ri Pak, asked if she was nervous before winning the U.S. Open*

NEW YORK, NEW YORK

"I love to wake up to garbage trucks and gunshots."

> *Diane Dixon, runner, on training in her hometown of Brooklyn*

"I know New York is an expensive city to live in. Maybe this can go toward a down payment someplace."

Martina Navratilova, after winning the U.S. Open and having combined winnings for the year of more than $6 million

O, CANADA

"It's like living in Green Bay with the Packers."
Cammi Granato, U.S. Olympic hockey team member, on the pressure of playing in Canada

OLYMPICS

"Losing the Olympic record is kind of bad, but I'm glad I lost it to an American."
Chandra Cheesborough, on losing the 400 meters to Valerie Brisco-Hooks

"These Olympics, probably more than ever before, are showing a lot of little girls it's OK to sweat, it's OK to play hard, it's OK to be an athlete."

Lindsay Davenport, on the significance of the '96 games

"I could have won a medal in five events if they let me."

Babe Didrikson, on being allowed to participate in only three events in the '32 games

"The unity of the athletes was the biggest high. It was almost like we came together as one."

Lisa Fernandez, U.S. Olympian softball pitcher, on the impact of women's sports in the '96 Olympics

"The Olympics is an incredible opportunity, but it's like anything else: whoever wins a race is just having a better day."

Juliana Fuptado, Olympic cyclist

"Where I come from, winning an Olympic medal is bigger than beating Martina Navratilova in the U.S. Open."

Zina Garrison

"The sun was shining. Everything was there. It was one great feeling."

> *Florence Griffith-Joyner, on her*
> *miraculous '88 Olympics*

"I can tell you, as a guy, how refreshing it is to see women on TV swimming, playing tennis, and horseback riding and not telling you how fresh they feel."

> *Jay Leno, on the '96 Olympics*

"When I stepped onto the ice, I knew what the Olympic experience is. It's a feeling of pure joy, and I put it in my program."

> *Tara Lipinski*

"All kids dream of being in the Olympics, not to mention in their own country. But being on Letterman: that's something I never imagined."

> *Rebecca Lobo*

"I didn't want Chris going to Seoul with all those strange men."

> *Pete Pfitzinger, on making the U.S.*
> *Olympic marathon team after his*
> *wife made the New Zealand Olympic*
> *team*

"The United States is no longer a follower in world gymnastics; we are a leader."

Mary Lou Retton, on the United States winning its first overall team gold medal in the '96 Olympics

"It's not a dream, because it's something I never even thought was possible. It's something I wouldn't have even dreamed about."

Pam Shriver, on playing on the first U.S. Olympic tennis team

"I think the best show in town is the Olympics, and I go to lots of other events. But like any other red-blooded female, I'm sure I'll get there."

Pam Shriver, on making shopping a priority at the Seoul Olympics

"I'm hoping some of the speed comes up through the floor and suddenly I've found myself very agile and quick on the court."

Pam Shriver, on living below the track and field contenders in the Olympic Village

"I'm staying in my first coed dorm. You don't get that kind of luxury in the women's tour."

Pam Shriver, on the advantages of being on the '88 Olympic team

"There's a rush of adrenalin from this. There's such beauty when she pulls it off, but there's that danger, too."

Dick Stone, father of Olympic aerial skier Nikki Stone

"I learned a lot about life here—everything is not Cinderella."

Debi Thomas, on finishing a disappointing third in the '88 Olympics

"They see athletics as one of the few places they have a chance to be number one, where they are judged purely on merit and their sex matters not in the least."

Paul Wylie, U.S. skater, on why women seem to do better in the Olympics than men

OPERA

"I wish I'd been a really great tennis player."

Marilyn Horne, opera singer, on her regrets in life

"All I know is that I've seen enough *Carmen*. I'm not going to see the opera."

Elizabeth Manley, on competing in the '88 Olympics against two favorites, Katarina Witt and Debi Thomas, who both chose to skate in the finals to the opera Carmen

OPPOSITION

"All I ever see is my opponent. You could set off dynamite in the next court, and I wouldn't notice."

Maureen Connolly

PAIN

"If it comes down to a choice between causing pain or taking it, I'll take it."
Mary Decker

PAIRS SKATING

"He presented her so beautifully, like a cherished little sister. They are everything pairs skating should be."
Sandra Bezic, on Ekaterina Gordeeva and Sergei Grinkov

"If my partner made a mistake, I'd want to kill him."
Michelle Kwan, on why she would never do pairs skating

"No, not yet. I have many years left. I am just starting. But I have a good start."

Se Ri Pak, asked if she considers herself the best player on the LPGA tour

"She seems to be one of those athletes who transcend their sport."

Jim Ritts, former LPGA commissioner

PARADES

"What have I done? All I have done is run fast. I do not see why people should make such a fuss."

Fanny Blankers-Koen, 1948 Olympic gold medalist, on a parade for her in Amsterdam

PENALTY SHOT

"I'll take a two-shot penalty, but I'll be damned if I'm going to play the ball where it lies."

> *Elaine Johnson, LPGA pro, after her*
> *shot hit a tree and rebounded into*
> *her bra*

PETS

"I'm getting a rabbit when I go home, and I'm going to name him Silver. And I think I'm going to get another one and name him Gold."

> *Amanda Beard, 14-year-old U.S.*
> *swimmer, after winning gold and*
> *silver medals*

"I talk to them every day. I must, every day and night. I call, and they tell me, 'We miss you.'"

> *Steffi Graf, on her German shepherds*

"An underdog can have a vicious bite."

> *Amy Van Dyken, on being an*
> *underdog in a swimming event*

POLICE

"The best six months of my life. You're taking people down at gunpoint all the time. I loved it."
Shannon Miller, Canadian women's hockey coach, on her prior job as a police officer

POLITICS

"I don't lie well enough to be a politician."
Rebecca Lobo, asked if she would capitalize on her fame by running for office in Connecticut

"Yeah, and I hope they get asked if they're related to Pam."
Pam Shriver, Republican, asked if she is related to the prominent Democratic Shriver family

POLLUTION

"I had scheduled four cars to back up to our practice gym. But Ursinus College [in Pennsylvania] wouldn't let us do it."

Vonnie Gros, U.S. women's field hockey coach, on trying to replicate the smog for their games at the '84 Olympics in Los Angeles

POOL SCHOOL

"I was lucky. Suppose my father had put in a tennis court instead. I can't play tennis at all."

Summer Sanders, on her dad's building a pool in their backyard

PRACTICE

"I stayed in the bunker until I made one. They had to bring me cocktails and dinner."

JoAnne Carner, on perfecting her sand game

"How many times can you go out there and do it, do it, do it, without once in a while having a bad go?"

Frank Carroll, Michelle Kwan's coach, on a bad practice before the Nationals

"I trained hard for this. I haven't gotten drunk since New Year's Eve. I haven't smoked since New Year's Eve. I was a serious, dedicated skater, and look what happened."

Mary Docter, U.S. speed skater, on finishing 18th in the Olympics

"We are not in the gym to be having fun. The fun comes in the end, with the winning of the medals."

Bela Karolyi, on his harsh training techniques

"They [spectators] don't realize all the work that's behind a good shot, and that your performance generally reflects how much practice has gone into it."

Billie Jean King

"Olympic medals are the real reward in my line of work."

Debbie Meyer, U.S. swimmer and
gold medal winner

"You should be able to do your entire routine sound asleep in your pajamas without one mistake. That's the secret. It's got to be a natural reaction."
Mary Lou Retton

"You see the cards, and you know the pain that is there. You need the payoff somewhere."

Summer Sanders, on practice cards

PREGNANT PAUSE

"She told me she was going to have eight whether I was the father or not."

Bobby Cole, husband of LPGA
pro Laura Baugh, mother of
seven children

"That putt was so good, I could feel the baby applaud."

> *Donna Horton-White, after sinking a 25-foot putt while seven months pregnant*

"I have no apologies. She might have been on the Olympic team, but I kicked her butt today."

> *Bruce Mosbacher, rugby player, on beating his wife, Nancy Ditz, in a marathon when she was seven months pregnant*

PRESSURE

"Never hurry when it counts."

> *JoAnne Carner*

"It was like going to an execution."

> *Dorothy Hamill, on the pressure of going out onto the ice*

"I was always taught to—or raised that way—that I always have pressure on myself. The harder, the better."

Martina Hingis

PRIVACY

"I love it here in the United States. In Japan, I have no privacy. In the States, I can have a hole in my jeans and nobody will notice."

Ayako Okamato, LPGA pro

PSYCH JOB

"I was so alert. I could feel the water in my hair in the shower. I would pick up my tennis racket thinking of nothing but picking up my tennis racket."

Billie Jean King, on getting psyched up before a big match

PUTTING

"Every putt can go in, but I don't expect every putt to go in."

Jane Blalock

"If it's my day, they go in, and on a bad day, they won't."

Laura Davies, on her putting philosophy

RECORDS

"It was unbelievable. I couldn't even drive, yet I had a world record."

Janet Evans, on breaking the 800-meters record at age 15

"I don't have to choose; I'll take all the records."

Marion Jones, asked what records she wanted

RELIGION

"I made peace with my own God and the local Gods."

> *Frank Carroll, Michelle Kwan's*
> *coach, on going to church and*
> *Japanese temples before the '98*
> *figure skating finals*

"She's going to worship the Lord instead of the swoosh."

> *Friend of Gwen Torrence, on*
> *Torrence's going to church instead of*
> *attending a Nike press conference*

RETIREMENT

"I haven't wanted to dream the next dream until this one was finished."

> *Anne Abernathy, "Grandma Luge,"*
> *competing at age 44 in the Olympics,*
> *on when she planned on retiring*

"It was no tragedy. It wasn't like I left behind this great legacy."

Mary Carillo, on being forced to retire from professional tennis

"I'm not going to even think about it until I shoot my address. I live at 30-30 South Ocean Boulevard."

JoAnne Carner, asked if she planned to retire at age 60

"As long as I am improving, I will go on, and besides, there's too much money in the business to quit."

Babe Didrikson, asked if she would retire after winning every golf tournament

"I'm sure she'll be spending some time doing what I've been doing—that is, being America's Guest."

Dan Jansen, asked what he thought Bonnie Blair would do in her retirement

"Why do people keep asking me if I'm going to quit? Did anyone ask Rubinstein when he was going to stop playing the piano?"
 Billie Jean King

"Sleep in for about two years."
 Julie Krone, on what she planned on doing after her retirement from horse racing

"You talk to any athlete who has been there for a long time: it doesn't matter how much they have won. You want that one more chance."
 Martina Navratilova, nearing retirement

"I've been in the twilight of my career longer than most people have careers."
 Martina Navratilova

"It's the mind that tells you when to give up."
 Merlene Ottey, sprinter, in her mid-30s

"When you think of gymnastics, you think of a tiny, ponytailed girl. That's not me."
Mary Lou Retton

"If she were a tourist attraction, she'd be Niagara Falls."
Jack Whitaker

RIVALRIES

"I'm a woman."
Nicole Bobek, asked the difference between her skating and that of then 15-year-old Michelle Kwan

"I was tired of hearing "O, Canada." I had not heard our anthem played after a major tournament. I really wanted to hear it."
Lisa Brown-Miller, U.S. Olympic hockey team member, on the United States defeating Canada for the gold medal

"Nobody beats Natasha 18 straight times."

> *Bud Collins, on Natasha Zvereva's*
> *beating Steffi Graf after 17 straight*
> *losses*

"Natasha impersonated the Washington Generals while Graf was the Globetrotters."

> *Bud Collins, on Zvereva's finally*
> *defeating Graf*

"Every Dempsey has a Tunney. Every Ali has a Frazier."

> *Mike Estep, Martina Navratilova's*
> *coach, on her rivalry with*
> *Chris Evert*

"If we weren't number one and two in the world, I know we'd be very, very close."

> *Chris Evert, on herself*
> *and Navratilova*

"Jackie started all this stuff. She sets a record; and I've got to go out and get even."

> *Florence Griffith-Joyner, on her good-*
> *natured rivalry with sister-in-law*
> *Jackie Joyner-Kersee*

"I don't mean this to sound conceited, but I could play to 90 percent of my potential and still win most of my matches against the other players. With Martina and me, whoever wins has to play 100 percent."

Chris Evert

"I don't know, actually, how I won this match. Maybe because I always beat her."

Martina Hingis, on her fifth straight win over Monica Seles

"They are the Ali and Frazier of the women's long jump: you know they'll force the best out of each other."

Bob Kersee, on the long-jump rivalry between Jackie Joyner-Kersee and Heike Drechsler

"I don't miss seeing all those backhands going past me when I am at the net."

Martina Navratilova, asked if she would miss her rivalry with Chris Evert upon Evert's retirement

"I wish we could quit right now and never play each other again. I wish that we could end up even, believe it or not, because it's just not right for one of us to say we are better."

Martina Navratilova, on being tied
with Chris Evert at 30 wins apiece

"They want to hold on to what they've got, and we want to take away what they have. It's a turf war."

Ben Smith, U.S. women's Olympic
hockey coach, on fighting for the
gold medal against Canada

"We see them in our sleep."

Ben Smith, on the U.S. Olympic
hockey team's main rival—Canada

"We're not at war with each other; we're at war with ourselves."

Gwen Torrence, sprinter, on her
rivalry with Merlene Ottey

"Katarina dies at the end of hers, and I don't."

Debi Thomas, on her and Katarina
Witt both performing Carmen *in the*
'88 Olympics skating finals

"When you see us out there for 10 seconds, it's a war. But when it's over, it's over."

Gwen Torrence, on her rivalry with Gail Devers

RODEO

"We don't even get the quality clowns."

Lynn Jankowski, on the difference between men's and women's rodeo

ROLE MODELS

"Little girls need big girls to look up to."

Teresa Edwards, WNBA player

"I want a little boy to say, 40 years from now, 'I want to run like Marion Jones, not Carl Lewis or Michael Johnson.'"

Marion Jones, on wanting to be remembered as a great athlete, not a great female athlete

"If a young female sees my dreams and goals come true, they will realize their dreams and goals might also come true."

Jackie Joyner-Kersee

"Tennis has always been reserved for the rich, the white, the males—and I've always been playing to change all that."

Billie Jean King

"A lot of women compare themselves to me and would like to be like me. They look at me and say, 'She can cook, she can clean the house, she can do shopping, she can walk the streets.'"

Jeannie Longo, champion
French bicyclist

"I hope, when I stop, people will think that somehow I mattered."

Martina Navratilova

"I've been waiting to put a diamond in my nose . . . but I'm worried that I'm going to make it OK for all the little girls to have diamonds in their noses."

Picabo Street

"It's great because a lot of us had to identify with male athletes growing up. Now these little girls have us."

> *Tina Thompson, WNBA player, on*
> *being considered a role model*

"It's important that little girls and young women have role models. I view myself and our student athletes as role models."

> *Pat Summitt, legendary basketball*
> *coach at the University of Tennessee*

"We don't have anybody to look up to—positive female role models in sports. Now little girls can choose."

> *Sheryl Swoopes, WNBA star*

"Before, we were playing because we liked to play. Now it's more competition—I want to be Lisa Leslie, I want to be Sheryl Swoopes."

> *Adrian Williams, college*
> *basketball star*

ROLLERBLADING

"People look at those skates and say, 'Hey, you're into Rollerblading,' and I'm not; I just don't like to walk."

Martina Navratilova

ROMANCE

"I certainly hope so."

Kate Schmidt, U.S. Olympic javelin team member, on whether there would be any fooling around in the Montreal Olympics despite strict rules

ROYALTY

"Thank you, Mary."

Louise Brough, on opponent Pauline Betz's being shaken when Queen Mary came to center court in Wimbledon to see them play

"I didn't know who they were. I shouldn't say this, but I was thinking, 'Couldn't they wait till the changeover?'"

> *Jennifer Capriati, on the arrival of*
> *King Juan Carlos and Queen Soffia*
> *during her match against Arantxa*
> *Sanchez Vicario in the Olympics*

"When I found out who he was, I said, 'Oh, yeah, he can come in any time.'"

> *Jennifer Capriati, on King Juan*
> *Carlos's coming in late to watch*
> *the match*

"I don't want to be a Dame. I'm no lady at all."

> *Laura Davies, asked if she*
> *were royalty*

"She didn't know how to curtsy. So, we had to rehearse that a few times in the waiting room."

> *Chris Evert, on teaching her*
> *opponent Corina Karlsson how to*
> *greet Princess Diana at center court*

"The only thing I've noticed is that when I come into the locker room, they all bow."

Martina Navratilova, on her opponents' being intimidated by her

"Nah, I've had enough practice."

Martina Navratilova, asked if she had to practice her curtsies before the Royal Box at Wimbledon

RUFFIAN

"I could cut through the infield, and she'd still beat me."

Braulio Baeza, on his horse's losing by a wide margin to the great filly Ruffian

RULES

"You have to play by the rules of golf just as you have to live by the rules of life. There's no other way."

Babe Didrikson, on life

"I've got to stretch the rules because I am special. . . . Rules are obstacles, things that get in the way of where I want to go."

Picabo Street

RUNNING

"I honestly think of running as an art form. Watching a great race is like looking at a pretty picture."

Mary Decker

"What makes running a joy for me is that it's not a duty or a responsibility or an obligation. It's just something I look forward to."

Sue Grafton, writer

"Luckily this isn't the Olympic Trials, or it would be a disaster. I'll take this as a learning experience."

Suzy Hamilton, on celebrating a lap early, thinking she had won a 1,500-meter race

"Sometimes people recognize me on the street when I'm running and want to stop and talk. I tell them, 'I don't mind talkin', but you've got to run with me because I'm not gonna stop.'"

Kathy Mattea, country singer

GABRIELA SABATINI

"She is a great human being. Yes, her personality has probably hurt her career, but in the long run, you want to be a good human being."

Juan Nunez, Sabatini's coach

ARANTXA SANCHEZ VICARIO

"The Barcelona Bumblebee."
Bud Collins

"She was running down balls only the Bionic Woman could get."
Werdel Witmeyer, her opponent in a tournament

SCHOOL DAYS

"I was the third-fastest sprinter on the track team—the boys' track team."
Evelyn Ashford, on running in high school

"Back when I was into guides, everybody but me had a 4.0 grade point average in high school."
Mary Carillo, on the embellishment of tennis media guides

"They know I'm not ditching."

> *Lindsay Davenport, asked if her*
> *teachers get mad at her when she*
> *misses school because she is playing*
> *on the tour*

"It's not like millions of people don't graduate from high school every year."

> *Lindsay Davenport, on being*
> *regarded as well educated in*
> *tennis because she graduated*
> *from high school*

"I'll make it up in the summer."

> *Tara Lipinski, on missing*
> *homework assignments during*
> *the Winter Olympics*

"I hate homework."

> *Maureen "Peanuts" Louie, on why*
> *she became a tennis pro at age 18*

"Do you believe after all this, I've got to go back to high school?"

> *Angela Ruggiero, 18-year-old U.S.*
> *Olympic hockey team player, after*
> *the United States won the gold medal*

"I'm allergic to bad grades. I once got a 60 on a test. After a match, I've never cried; after that test, I cried."

Venus Williams

"Go to summer school."

Venus Williams, on what she would do after losing her first-round match at Wimbledon

BRIANA SCURRY

"Playing against Briana is like rock climbing a slab of marble. There are no weaknesses in her game."

Jim Budy, Scurry's soccer coach at the University of Massachusetts

SECOND PLACE

"Sometimes in second place, you look up and see only how short a step it is to get to first. But in first, sometimes you look back and see how far you can fall."

> *Richard Callaghan, coach of Tara Lipinski, on advantages she had being in second place going into the finals against Michelle Kwan*

"When you've been second best for so long, you can either accept it or try to become the best."

> *Florence Griffith-Joyner, on always finishing second*

"My husband told me he read *War and Peace* between Lorraine's finish and mine."

> *Suzanne Ray, on finishing a distant second to Lorraine Moller in a race*

"She's got a lot in common with . . . Jimmy Connors—a dynamic fighter with heart who feeds off a good crowd."
Mary Carillo

"It's Steffi's forehand off both sides."
Chris Evert

"I'd rather be playing Monica Seles."
Martina Navratilova, on being forced to testify in the Judy Nelson palimony suit

"She beat me, and I ain't no slouch potato."
Martina Navratilova, on Seles's comeback after injury

"What ticks me off is seeing how much the seniors are making playing on Mickey Mouse golf courses, shooting 20 under par."

> *Helen Alfredsson, on the disparity*
> *between the LPGA and the*
> *senior tour*

"America loves power. I'd rather see someone hit it 350 yards off the tee, too. But I'd rather watch us than the seniors."

> *Juli Inkster, on the LPGA*

SERVES

"Yours, too."

> *Waiter at a restaurant, to Martina*
> *Navratilova after she said his service*
> *was excellent*

"Every time I hit a big serve, it was overseas. I'm getting better at converting in my mind, but it was nice to see it here."

> *Venus Williams, on converting her*
> *speedy serves from kilometers into*
> *miles per hour*

"There might be someone who comes bigger than me and taller and who has a better form, but I don't think it's going to happen."

> *Venus Williams, asked if she thought*
> *anyone could serve faster than her*
> *125 mph record*

PATTY SHEEHAN

"There's no such thing as the 'best' golf swing. Sheehan's just looks like it ought to be."

> *Tom Boswell*

"To watch Patty Sheehan swing a golf club is to witness the gift of natural grace."

> *Jaime Diaz*

"Guts and nerves of steel. And a touch of softness."
> *Kathy Johnson, Olympic silver
> medalist in gymnastics, on what it
> takes to win*

"It's been tough. Now it's over, I can finally say it.
I've felt as if I've been in prison."
> *Nancy Kerrigan, on winning the
> silver medal in the '94 Olympics*

"No, it's not the color medal I wanted, but I'll
take it."
> *Michelle Kwan, on her second-place
> finish to Tara Lipinski*

SISSI

"When you look up in the sky at night and see all
the constellations, there is one star that shines
brighter."
> *Wilson Rica, coach of the Brazilian
> national team, on the great Sissi*

SKIING

"Nothing. Skiing is my life. That's what I like to do."

Debbie Armstrong, Olympic gold medal winner, on the sacrifices she made for skiing

SKYDIVING

"If you jumped out of an airplane, somehow managed to land on the tee, and then hit a drive, you probably would hit it 400 yards."

Karrie Webb, LPGA pro, on how skydiving pumps her up

SLICE

"Well, there must be a bottle of scotch over there in those bushes."

Babe Didrikson, on consistently slicing her golf shots to the right

SNEAKERS

"Once I start to run, I forget what I have on my feet, anyway. Whoops, there goes the endorsement."
Holli Hyche, Indiana State runner,
on winning a race in borrowed shoes

SOCCER

"I never thought there would be this many people to watch me do anything, let alone play soccer. It's a great thing for women's sports."
Briana Scurry, on the more than
75,000 fans at the women's soccer
finals in the '96 Olympics

"This is a women's soccer school. We're just trying to keep up with them."
Dean Smith, legendary basketball
coach at North Carolina, on the
North Carolina women's soccer team
that has won more than 15 national
championships in the last two
decades

"**M**y girls have not exhibited signs of indiscipline. We believe in attacking football, not negative play."
Ismaila Mabo, Nigerian soccer coach, in preparation for playing the United States in the 1999 World Cup

SOCIAL LIFE

"**I**'ve got a friend who is a nun, and she has a better social life than I have."
Wendy Turnbull

SOFTBALL

"**I** tried the Brownies, but I didn't like the skirt."
Candace Murray, Canadian Olympic softball player, on why she took up the sport

"I think we'll never be the same. My cleats never touched the ground."

> *Dot Richardson, on the United States*
> *winning the gold medal in softball*
> *in 1996*

ANNIKA SORENSTAM

"The way she's playing, if I finish one shot ahead of Annika this week, I'm going to consider it a good week, probably be holding that trophy."

> *Laura Davies*

SPEED

"I want to go down in history as the fastest woman who's ever been on earth."

> *Marion Jones*

"There's no room for fear with speed. They don't coincide."

> *Picabo Street*

"God just gave us a little more speed, but on the day of the finals, one of us will have to be faster than the rest."

Gwen Torrence, on competing in the Olympic finals with Evelyn Ashford and others

"I like the idea of being the world's fastest woman. There's not another title like it. A distance runner can't be the world's longest runner."

Gwen Torrence

"I love the feeling of going fast."

Sheila Young, on why she competes in speed skating

SPONSORS

"In 1984, my shoe sponsor said it would take care of me for life. I guess I died in 1988."

Ruth Wysocki, professional runner, on the end of her shoe contract

SPORTS COMPARISONS

"I'm not saying I can do what Tracy Austin does, but then, Tracy doesn't have to hit backhands with an elbow in her face, either."

> *Nancy Lieberman, on her salary of*
> *$100,000 for playing basketball*
> *compared with half a million made*
> *by Tracy Austin in tennis*

"Figure skating is different from, say, football, where you have an opponent and you can affect their scoring. I have to go out and give my personal-best performance every time."

> *Kristi Yamaguchi*

SPORTS WISDOM

"Gone are the days when women's sports were simply tolerated. Now they're celebrated."

> *Val Ackerman, WNBA commissioner*

"I believe that sports is a birthright."

> *Anita DeFrantz, 1980 Olympic rower*

SPOUSES

"I can still beat my husband—but I could beat him when I was nine months pregnant."

> *Chris Evert, on playing husband*
> *Andy in tennis after their son*
> *was born*

"When I win, call me Evert. When I lose, call me Lloyd."

> *Chris Evert, on the correct form for*
> *her name after her marriage to*
> *John Lloyd*

"I'll know it's time to quit when she wins one. I've never lost."

> *Bob Kersee, on arguments with his*
> *wife, Jackie Joyner-Kersee*

"I'm the only man alive whose wife approves of him going around with fast women."

> *Ed Temple, Tennessee State women's*
> *track coach*

DAWN STALEY

"It's like she has six eyes on the court."

*Maynell Meadors, WNBA coach, on
Staley's great passing ability*

"As a player, you've got to have your hands and
eyes ready all the time. She'll get it there."

Rebecca Lobo

STEEPLECHASE

"You make one spill or hit a barrier, and you may
as well get a job at Burger King."

*Carla Borovicka, women's 2,000-
meter steeplechase record holder*

GEORGE STEINBRENNER

"That's nice. I just bought a T-shirt."

Heidi Voelker, U.S. Olympic skier, on running into Steinbrenner at the Olympics, where he told her he just bought a hockey team

STREAKS

"You take it when you get it, and right now I'm gettin' it."

Beth Daniels, LPGA Hall of Famer, on a hot streak

PICABO STREET

"There's a lot better technical skiers out there, but Picabo has the mental strength to pull up every fiber in her body for the win."

Paul Major, U.S. skiing official

"I always said I had to keep her brother fed and Picabo alive."

> *Dee Street, on her daughter's being a daredevil at a young age*

"Before, I was a pain in the ass. Now I'm merely eccentric."

> *Picabo Street, on her changes over the last few years*

"I credit myself."

> *Picabo Street, on whom she credits for her victories*

STRENGTHS

"Now they say I'm too strong and too fast. Well, I'm not going to feel sorry for those people. They're just going to have to raise their game up to mine."

> *Martina Navratilova, on excuses offered by her opponents*

"I thought it was the greatest, most inspiring, most motivating thing I've ever seen."

> *Tim Daggett, Olympic gymnast, on*
> *Kerri Strug's vault in the Olympics*
> *after she was injured*

"You'll never see Kerri on a Wheaties box."

> *Bela Karolyi, on Strug's lack of*
> *notoriety before the '96 Olympics*

"She had the gold, the silver, the bronze in her hand. She had the whole team's destiny in her hand."

> *Bela Karolyi, on Strug's famous jump*
> *in the '96 games*

"If that was me and I had a broken neck, I would have done it because this is a once-in-a-lifetime opportunity."

> *Bela Karolyi, on Strug's jump*

"Success means to me always striving for a personal best. You don't have to be in first, second, or third place in order to taste success."
Bonnie Blair

"They say they've taken up a collection to send me on a three-week vacation."
> *Nancy Lopez, on how the other members of the LPGA were responding to her amazing success at the age of 21*

"When I win, it is routine. When I lose, life comes to an end."
> *Martina Navratilova, at the height of her success*

"My success was totally up to me. I didn't do it for the galleries or money. Playing well was self-gratifying."
> *Kathy Whitworth, LPGA pro*

PAT SUMMITT

"She is to women's basketball what John Wooden was to men's basketball."

> *Don Meyer, college basketball*
> *coach, on Summitt's brilliant*
> *career at Tennessee*

SWEAT

"It's OK for a woman to perspire. I still like flowers."

> *Juli Inkster*

SWIMMING

"My family and coach said to think of this as a big party with a swim meet attached."

> *Amanda Beard, on participating in*
> *the Olympics at age 14*

"I like to be able to put on perfume and not have this chlorine smell to it."

> *Amy Van Dyken, on why she wanted to take a break from swimming*

"I didn't pick it—it picked me."

> *Mary T. Meagher, on swimming the fly since age four*

"Swimming is the only sport you can do from your first bath to your last, without hurting yourself. You are ageless and weightless in the water."

> *Esther Williams*

SWINGERS

"My swing is no uglier than Arnold Palmer's, and it's the same ugly swing every time."

> *Nancy Lopez*

"The average player is too anxious to see good results on the scoreboard before she has fully absorbed the principles of the golf swing in mind and muscle on the practice tee."

> *Louise Suggs*

"No matter how powerful your engine, you must have gradual acceleration of speed. So it is in a golf swing."

Mickey Wright

SHERYL SWOOPES

"You don't appreciate Sheryl Swoopes until you try to stop her."

Nancy Darsch, Ohio State coach,
on Swoopes's scoring 47 points
against them

SYNCHRONIZED SWIMMING

"It's not sports; it's showbiz."

Avery Brundage, Olympic Games
president

"Try running a five-minute mile and holding your breath for two-thirds of it."

> Gail Emery, U.S. synchronized swim
> coach, on how good an athlete you
> have to be to participate in the sport

"Now, take the phrase 'solo synchronized swimming': it just don't make sense. If you're all by yourself, who are you going to synchronize with?"

> Gallagher

"You have to be fairly attractive and have a good body to be successful. I mean, if the judges don't want to look at you for five minutes, it doesn't matter if you look good."

> Carolyn Waldo, Canadian
> synchronized swimmer

"It's a grueling sport . . . you have to train for years; you have to be precise, skilled, and athletic."

> Esther Williams

TAX MAN

"I don't even think about first place. The IRS takes all of it, anyway."

Laura Baugh, on finishing second a great deal on the LPGA tour

TEMPER, TEMPER

"My original dream was to play golf well enough to be allowed to throw my clubs."

JoAnne Carner

"If guys do it, it's macho, and if women do it, it's not very nice."

Wendy Turnbull, on bad conduct

"The only mature thing I see in some players is their tennis."

> *Mary Carillo, on young girls joining*
> *the pro tennis tour*

"The rules of tennis are fine, as far as I'm concerned. Except, perhaps, for that whole curtsy thing."

> *Mary Carillo, on players having to*
> *curtsy on center court in Wimbledon*

"Tennis is like marrying for money: love means nothing."

> *Phyllis Diller*

"Tennis to me is just like a chess game. You have to maneuver; you have to know your opponents' strengths and weaknesses."

> *Althea Gibson*

"I love that the ball doesn't come over the net twice the same way in a lifetime, and that I'm always in the process of finding new shots."

> *Billie Jean King*

"A perfect combination of violent action taking place in an atmosphere of total tranquility."
>   *Billie Jean King*

"I wanted a sport where I could still be considered feminine. That hasn't been easy. . . . Hopefully, no longer are we regarded as muscle-bound, Amazonian jerks."
>   *Billie Jean King, on athletic stereotypes, 1972*

"When I grow up, I am going to learn how to play tennis."
>   *Tara Lipinski, at age 15*

"So I lied."
>   *Martina Navratilova, on having said early in her career that no one woman could dominate tennis*

"If you see a tennis player who looks as if he is working very hard, then that means he isn't very good."
>   *Helen Wills Moody*

"Tennis is like football: you must set up the plays. If you set it up right, all you have to do is execute."

Martina Navratilova

"My short game in golf is bad, but it's pretty good in tennis."

Wendy Turnbull, tennis pro

TIME FRAMES

"I realize most people in the world have to be at work by 8:30, but I'm glad the final's starting at 2."

Martina Hingis, on being forced to play a Wimbledon match at 8:30 A.M.

TITLE IX

"I have a son and a daughter. I want both of them to have opportunities. But I don't want my daughter to feel guilty because she's made to believe she's keeping boys from playing sports."

Donna de Varona, on Title IX's providing a more level playing field for women in collegiate sports

TOENAILS

"It kind of reminds me, every time I see my toes, what I'm doing here."

Tricia Dunn, U.S. Olympic hockey team player, on painting her toenails gold

"I wish they wouldn't grow back. Evolution hasn't caught up with us. We don't need toenails. We aren't digging anymore."

Sue Olsen, ultramarathoner, on toenails being a major deterrent to her running

TOMBOY

"You're just an athlete, not a man or a woman. I think it's important to note that there is no word for *tomboy* in the Czech language."

> *Martina Navratilova, on the muscularity of her fellow Czech female athlete, runner Jarnila Kratochvilovi*

GWEN TORRENCE

"Gwen's the Charles Barkley of track. She speaks out just like he does."

> *Manley Waller, Torrence's husband, on her controversial views*

TRAINING

"You have to avoid dancing too much, and going to the movies too often."

> *Maureen Connolly, on training tactics*

UNDERWEAR

"I spent the whole day worrying about whether someone would see my underwear."

> *Nancy Lopez, blaming a second-place finish on a broken zipper*

"I couldn't have caused more of a stir if I had walked out there naked."

> *Gussie Moran, on wearing lace panties at Wimbledon in 1949*

"Is that where you'd like to have your underwear?"

> *Gussie Moran, to Ted Tinling after he requested the lace panties for the tennis Hall of Fame*

"It is almost impossible to comprehend how a yard of lace added to a player's normal undergarment, barely visible, caused such a furor."

> *Ted Tinling, the creator of the lace panties*

U.S. OPEN (GOLF)

"I wish it could have been a 54-hole tournament, the last 54."

> *JoAnne Carner, on losing the U.S. Women's Golf Open by only a few strokes after a first-round 81*

"A win."

> *Dale Eggeling, asked after going 0-for-19 in the U.S. Open what would make the 20th different*

"Yes. And getting more and more, too."

> *Se Ri Pak, asked if she was the most famous woman in Korea after winning the U.S. Open*

U.S. OPEN (TENNIS)

"Wimbledon is special, peaceful. Here is like a zoo."

> *Hana Mandlikova*

"They acted like Yankee fans."

Martina Navratilova, on rowdy fans
at the U.S. Open in Queens

U.S. WOMEN'S
SOCCER TEAM

"We're at the epicenter of a big rock being thrown into a huge pond. We don't know what the ripple effect will be."

Michelle Akers, on the United States
winning the World Cup

"It kind of makes sense that we're at Disneyland. This whole thing is a fantasy."

Brandi Chastain, on the U.S. team's
celebration after winning the
World Cup

"We're women who like to knock people's heads off and then put on a skirt and go dancing."

Brandi Chastain

"I think the whole country was caught up in this, not only fans of soccer, but young girls. In some ways, it is the biggest sporting event of the last decade."

President Clinton, on the
1999 World Cup

"They have shown us that when we reach back to look for what we've always loved about sports— teamwork, humility, and sportsmanship—it's still there."

Donna de Varona

"It's a new sound to the great stadiums of the world. It's higher pitched."

Donna de Varona, on all the female
fans at the U.S. women's soccer
team games

"It's a storybook ending for a team that has its place in history."

Tony DiCicco, coach

"They are this year's Spice Girls, only with more talent."

John Donovan, sports columnist

"I don't know if it's the Spice Girls or the Backstreet Boys or the Beatles or what."

Richard Finn, public relations director of the World Cup, on the huge crowds following the U.S. team

"Just the fact that now they can finally watch women doing great things on the field in front of great crowds."

Julie Foudy, on the greatest thing about the U.S. win

"I think people are going to look back and say that this changed the way they look at women's athletics."

Julie Foudy

"We've always said this team is America's best-kept secret. So, finally the secret's out."

Julie Foudy

"Hot-blooded babes with a lot of physical energy."

Julie Foudy, describing the U.S. World Cup team

"Babe City."

David Letterman, describing the U.S. World Cup team

"This movement is more than a game. It's about female athletes. It's about sports. It's about everything."

Kristine Lilly, on the significance of the U.S. victory

"The legacy I want to leave is that no longer can anyone take women athletics lightly."

Tiffeny Milbrett

"I don't think you have to run around naked to sell the game, but it's good at least to be in the minds of people. I don't think it's undignified."

Briana Scurry, on Brandi Chastain's taking her shirt off after scoring the goal to win the World Cup

"The queen mother doesn't have enough money to pay these women what they deserve right now."

Hank Steinbrecher, general secretary of the U.S. Soccer Federation, on the impact of the team

"The most popular traveling band since the Grateful Dead."

Grant Wahl

VICTORY

"The moment of victory is much too short to live for that and nothing else."

Martina Navratilova

VIDEO

"It's not like I'm going to whip it out at a party or anything."

Briana Scurry, on having a video of herself running naked after the U.S. women's team won the gold medal in the '96 Olympics

VIVE LA FRANCE

"I feel French."

Steffi Graf, asked how she felt after
winning the French Open

VOLLEYBALL

"When it all works well, it feels like heaven. That's
the best way I can describe it. You feel like you're
playing a song."

Flo Hyman, on the U.S. women's
Olympic volleyball team

"In men's volleyball, it's just boom, boom, boom.
Power. The women have to win by skill and by
outsmarting their opponents; it requires more
finesse, more sophistication."

Arie Selinger, U.S. women's Olympic
volleyball coach

"It would increase our attendance with just the Secret Service."

> *Don Shaw, Stanford women's volleyball coach, asked what would happen if Chelsea Clinton played on the team*

GRETE WAITZ

"A New Yorker by adoption."

> *Ed Koch, former NYC mayor, following Waitz's great success in the New York Marathon*

WARDROBE

"I don't know, but I'm sure not going to find it in Butte."

> *Bonnie Blair, attending college in Butte, Montana, on what she would wear to an awards dinner honoring her and Flo Jo*

"She's become a Slav to fashion."
> *Kim Cunningham, on Martina*
> *Navratilova's love of clothes*

"We're here to skate in a dress and not a G-string. All that's missing is the horses and the reins. It's a circus."
> *Peter Dunfield, Elizabeth Manley's*
> *coach, on Katarina Witt's skating*
> *outfits*

"Colors excite me. Sprinting is excitement."
> *Florence Griffith-Joyner, on why it's*
> *important to her to be flamboyant on*
> *the track*

"Those are our uniforms; that's our office. It'd be difficult to play in panty hose and pumps."
> *Linda Hanley, U.S. women's beach*
> *volleyball player, on wearing bathing*
> *suits while playing*

"I know it wasn't great. . . . You don't see yourself on the court."
> *Martina Hingis, on wearing a skirt*
> *with bicycle shorts*

"**M**y dress was already ready for the picture with the trophy."

> *Martina Hingis, upset after losing the French Open final to Steffi Graf*

"**G**ood-clothes sports."

> *Billie Jean King, on the only sports in which women could participate— tennis, skating, and golf*

"**W**e should all try to look more ladylike on the course. Being thought of as anything but a woman definitely frosts me."

> *Carol Mann*

"**I**t wasn't as though she didn't have a bra on. It certainly would be discrimination to suggest a women can't do it if a man does."

> *Roger Rogers, editor of* Women's Soccer, *on Brandi Chastain's ripping her shirt off after scoring the winning goal in the World Cup*

"When I found out it was reality, I thought it was a stroke of genius."

> *Dick Versace, Indiana Pacers coach, on being told that Florence Griffith-Joyner was hired to create new Pacers uniforms*

"The costumes that enhance the music: I think this is very important. When I wear the right costumes, I feel much better. Why not stress what we have that is attractive?"

> *Katarina Witt*

"I think every man prefers looking at a well-built woman [rather] than someone built in the shape of a ball."

> *Katarina Witt, defending her choice of skating outfits*

WEATHER WATCH

"It was a perfectly normal English day."

> *Trish Johnson, LPGA player from Great Britain, on a miserable, rainy day*

"If the weather's good, you ski; if it's bad, you go
to school."

> *Andrea Mead, gold medal skier in
> the '52 Olympics, on life in Vermont*

"I got a couple of workouts in."

> *Karen Weiss, LPGA pro, on getting
> stronger in the off-season by
> shoveling snow in Minnesota*

KARRIE WEBB

"When she gets on a roll, there's no stopping her
from making a lot of birdies. All you can do is just
get out of her way."

> *Donna Andrews*

"Can you believe that little devil? I believe she is
the best ball striker in the world right now. I've
always thought that."

> *Jane Geddes*

"She has no weaknesses. I wish I had her on the President's Cup team. She'd give the men something to think about."

Peter Thomson, President's Cup captain

WEIGHTS

"If you want to run like a man, you have to train like a man."

Florence Griffith-Joyner, on lifting weights

"Now it's cool for a woman to be able to out–bench press her husband."

Amy Van Dyken

WEIGHTY ISSUES

"She was so wide that we could not tell if she were coming or going."

Bob Kersee, coach of Flo Jo, on her gaining a lot of weight in the early '80s

"Do you realize that between us, we've lost Laura Baugh?"

Stan Wood, USC golf coach, who lost 50 pounds, to JoAnne Carner, who lost 45 pounds

WHAT'S IN A NAME?

"Yeah, it makes me feel younger."

Chris Evert, asked if she liked being called Chrissie at age 25

"My dad always told me one day I'd be glad I had that name because people would always remember it, but I'm not sure that day has come yet."
Nancy Hogshead

"My grandma named me after Jacqueline Kennedy, hoping that someday I'd be the first lady of something."

Jackie Joyner-Kersee

"I'm enjoying everything except when people put Ms. on the envelope of my letters."

Kay Whitmore, NHL goalie

KATHY WHITWORTH

"When she had to putt, she got it every time."

Sandra Haynie

WILLIAMS SISTERS

"They're sheer power. They're going to knock the crap out of people. They're going to beat you up."

Nick Bollettieri, on Venus and Serena Williams

"Everything's working for them. They go for their shots, they're taking risks, and they don't really have a weakness."

Steffi Graf

"I'm more of a celebrity than the players. The only players I'm not more of a celebrity than are Venus and Serena, which is really amazing."

Richard Williams, father of the Williams sisters

"When Venus said her greatest adversary was going to be her sister, she wasn't kidding."

Richard Williams, on the play of Serena

"If UCLA can teach a monkey to answer the telephone, then you can teach a human being to do anything."

Richard Williams, on teaching Venus and Serena to play tennis at the age of four

"It's not that there aren't talented players here. It's just that my girls are better than they are."

Richard Williams, before 1999 U.S. Open (won by Serena)

"You beat my sister. I owe you."
> *Venus Williams, to Anne Miller after defeating her in a tournament*

"You know what I don't like about Venus? She's so much taller than I am. She can serve faster."
> *Serena Williams*

"What dream? It's reality waiting to happen."
> *Venus Williams, on the dream that she and her sister would be ranked number one and two in the world and number one in doubles*

"There's great satisfaction because she takes players down left and right. So, to survive such an onslaught is great."
> *Venus Williams, on how it felt defeating Serena*

"A Williams."
> *Venus Williams, on who would win a finals match between her and Serena*

"I'm not a follower, generally the leader. Sometimes others might choose to get on that path, but they have to get behind me. Everything I want, I usually get."

Venus Williams

WIMBLEDON

"Like, it's great in there. Like, you don't have any noise or anything. Then the seagulls fly over."

Carling Bassett, on playing in center court

"The tournament is in charge, and you are a guest in the house."

Mary Carillo

"There's something very special about this joint. It has that Augusta Masters feel about it."

Mary Carillo

"This court is her court."

Chris Evert, on Martina Navratilova's playing in center court

"This is where my heart is, no matter where in the world I am. I know and love every inch of that court. It's my place."

> Billie Jean King, on center court

"I'm going to eat grass to prepare for Wimbledon."

> Iva Majoli, on her problems on the grass courts of Wimbledon

"Just about every day, I think about tennis, and tennis is Wimbledon."

> Martina Navratilova

"They don't put an asterisk next to your name saying you won but didn't play that well."

> Martina Navratilova, on winning her ninth Wimbledon but being disappointed in her play

"I prefer to consider my love for Wimbledon a rational reverence."

> Martina Navratilova, on claims that she is obsessed with Wimbledon

"I feel this place in my bones. I feel all those champions out there, dead and alive, when I'm out there. There's no place like it."

Martina Navratilova

"It gives you confidence, not only for the next couple of weeks, but it gives you confidence for life."

Jana Novotna, on winning Wimbledon

"I was going to give England something exciting for once."

Serena Williams, on losing before having the opportunity to play her sister Venus at Wimbledon

WINNING

"I thought at this point in my life, I just wanted to accept the trophy with some dignity. But it's just not my style."

Amy Alcott, on keeping her tradition alive of jumping into water after a tournament win even at age 35

"You can't be scared to win. When you win, you let yourself win."

Amy Alcott

"The only thing I never learned from Billy Martin was how to knock a guy out in a bar."

JoAnne Carner, on how her friend Billy Martin helped teach her how to win

"My ambition is to play perfect tennis. Then I will always win."

Maureen Connolly

"I don't need a demotion."

Jody Conradt, University of Texas womens' basketball coach, asked after her winning season if she wanted to coach the men's team, which had a losing season

"I am out to beat everybody in sight, and that is just what I'm going to do."

Babe Didrikson

"When I race, my opponents are my opponents. If it were my best friend, once we were in the water, it would be an opponent. I just swim to win."
Janet Evans

"Once you've been number one, you can never be satisfied with less."
Chris Evert

"I think about what the other player's face would look like at the net if they beat me."
Chris Evert, on what motivates her to win

"Being a champ is all well and good, but you can't eat a crown."
Althea Gibson

"I know what I have to do, and I'm going to do whatever it takes. If I do it, I'll come out a winner, and it doesn't matter what anyone else does."
Florence Griffith-Joyner

"I hope now it's going to be easier for the next two or three matches."

> *Martina Hingis, on beating her*
> *first-round Wimbledon opponent,*
> *7–5, 6–3*

"The main thing is not a matter of wanting to win; the main thing is being scared to lose."

> *Billie Jean King*

"The best players, I think, are always the ones who remember the losses, because they remember the pain, and they hate it."

> *Billie Jean King*

"I've bowled maybe 25 times in my entire life, yet every time I went up to the line, I expected to knock all the pins down."

> *Billie Jean King*

"I have transcended another level."

> *Martina Navratilova, on winning four*
> *straight majors in singles and doubles*

"If you have pride in your game, you don't let opponents determine how you play."

> *Tara Van Derveer, former women's Olympic basketball coach*

"Winning is like going out and beating up on people. I get joy out of that."

> *Serena Williams*

KATARINA WITT

"Even though she's been trained like a robot, you can't train someone to have it. There's no question, she has it."

> *Robin Cousins*

WNBA

"If I find the right woman—notice what I said, the right woman—to coach this team, I'd step down tomorrow."

> *Frank Layden, on taking over as coach of the WNBA's Utah Starzz*

"The WNBA is a new goal for the 80 million girls and women who play basketball. There is no more dead end. Now they have a place to go."

Lynette Woodard

WOMEN, START YOUR ENGINES

"All of them, every single one of them, when they come to the starting line, they're afraid. Not because I'm a woman, but because they know we're good."

Shirley Muldowney

WOMEN'S SPORTS

"Women's team sports seem to be the purer form of what sports was originally supposed to be."

Kate Schmidt, U.S. Olympian

TIGER WOODS

"I would hope so. I'm tall. I'm black. Everything's different about me. Just face the facts."

Venus Williams, on being favorably compared to Tiger

WORLD CUP

"I felt like I was crushing diamonds in my lower intestines from the pressure."

Anson Dorrance, former U.S. World Cup soccer coach, on pressure during the 1991 World Cup

WORM

"We're not talking date here. The whole family is going out."

Dan Beard, father of 14-year-old gold medalist Amanda, on her plans to go out to breakfast with Dennis Rodman

"We're both assertive and know what we want. He's about doing what he wants, the same as me."
> *Lisa Leslie, comparing herself to*
> *Dennis Rodman*

MICKEY WRIGHT

"I didn't think anyone but the Babe could hit 'em like that."
> *Babe Didrikson, on the drives of then*
> *19-year-old Mickey Wright*

"Wright has the finest golf swing I ever saw, man or woman."
> *Ben Hogan*

"Mickey Wright was the best female player ever, bar none. And there's not even a second, third, or fourth."
> *Dave Marr*

"Mickey got the outside world to take a second look at women golfers, and when they looked, they saw the rest of us."
> *Judy Rankin*

"She set a standard of shot making that will probably never be equaled."
Betsy Rawls

KIM ZMESKAL

"Kim is so fierce inside. She's got a steel stomach and a steel heart."
Mary Lou Retton, on Zmeskal's gymnastic abilities

INDEX

Italicized page numbers indicate names
referred to in a quote. All other names are
actual sources of a quote.